SUNRISE C

Samuel Taylor Coleridge
&
Russell Lee Hawkins

Matador
5 Weir Road
Kibworth Beauchamp
Leicester LE8 0LQ, UK
Tel: 0116 279 2299
Email: books@troubador.co.uk
Web: www.troubador.co.uk/matador

ISBN 978 184876 541 2

British Library Cataloguing in Publication Data.
A catalogue record for this book is available from the British Library.

Typeset in 11pt Garamond by Troubador Publishing Ltd, Leicester, UK
Printed in the UK by TJ International Ltd, Padstow, Cornwall

Matador is an imprint of Troubador Publishing Ltd

For

Pat

Who stood shoulder to shoulder until the end.

&

"The man from Porlock"

May God bless him.

Foreword

James McKusick

Poetry by its origin is a spoken medium, and its best practitioners have always been those whose words are expressed by spoken voice, not merely encapsulated in silent print. As a poet, Russell Hawkins harks back to the remote origins of poetry, particularly in the oral traditions of the Norse and Celtic pre-literate societies, where the bards held positions of eminence - and his work comes most fully into its own as poetry of the spoken word. In this respect, his poetry has little to do with the impotent ivory tower of academic verse, and much more in common with the verve and gusto of the Spoken Word movement in contemporary poetry. One must hear these poems spoken aloud in order to realize their true lucidity and magnificence.

Poetry as performance is at the heart of what Hawkins seeks to accomplish in all of his work. Just as the ancient Celtic bards, by traveling from place to place, sought to create a living connection with their auditors through the recitation of traditional tales, so too Hawkins has spent many years in search of the ideal audience for the performative utterance of his verse. The present volume will certainly succeed in conveying his work to wider audience, but those who read it must carry firmly in mind the understanding that the poems published here emerge from a living oral tradition. For this reason, the reader must become a listener first and foremost.

I first met Russell Hawkins at the Coleridge Conference held in Somerset in July 2006, and on first hearing his work, I found it absolutely captivating. Hawkins recited his continuation of Coleridge's 'Kubla Khan' in a bold, emphatic manner, holding the undivided attention of all those present, and conveying something of the manner of Coleridge himself, for whom 'Kubla Khan' was a favorite set-piece, frequently recited aloud at social gatherings to the rapt attention of his listeners. The framing device of this poem relies upon the hypnotic presence of the bardic poet, as evoked by Coleridge's memorable lines, 'And all should cry, Beware! Beware! / His flashing eyes, his floating hair!' Any writer who seeks to compose a continuation of Coleridge's magical and mysterious poem 'Kubla Khan' needs first to confront the bardic legacy, the prophetic voice, and the oral-formulaic tradition evoked by Coleridge within the poem itself. By so doing, Hawkins has enabled his listener (or reader) to embark upon a shared journey of discovery, leading not to a dry, formal imitation of Coleridge's style, but to a much more fundamental re-imagining of the setting, the story, and the hypnotic quality of the recitation itself. The continuation of 'Kubla Khan' presented within these pages must be experienced as precisely such a re-imagining of the poem, taking the story in a direction that may (or may not) be precisely what Coleridge intended, but which certainly carries forward the bardic tradition of which Coleridge himself aspired to become a practitioner. In his continuation of this poem, Hawkins conveys the vital energy, the dreamlike quality, and the incantatory music of the original. Just as important, he picks up the poem's narrative thread precisely at the point where Coleridge left off, and brings it through mysterious, winding passages to a compelling, though unexpected, conclusion.

Hawkins takes a similar approach in his continuation of Coleridge's 'Ballad of the Dark Ladie', a somewhat lesser-known work that he treats with careful attention to detail, once again in a manner that seeks to push forward the creative spark or vital impetus that gave rise to the original poem. Using a free hand with characterization and voice, Hawkins weaves a narrative tapestry that takes its cues from the suggestive details of Coleridge's poem while also drawing upon the deep and complex lore of Arthurian romance. This poem, like much else that Hawkins writes, refuses to lie static upon the page. It will lay its deepest hold upon a reader who recites it aloud, and will find its fullest expression only in performative utterance. The subtle variation of stanza form, the incantatory repetition of key images, and the precise accordance of diction with particular characters, will become quite apparent in an oral recitation of this poem.

In his shorter, lyrical poems, Hawkins speaks most directly of his own experience, which has been a good deal more varied than the typical adolescent angst or mid-life crisis conveyed by many pallid and forgettable modern writers. As a former military officer, martial artist, and ski instructor, Hawkins has lived life to its core, seen things that many of us will never see, and lived to tell the tale. Not merely trading upon his past adventures, however, Hawkins seeks in his poetry to convey something much more subtle and profound. In the brutal emotional honesty of his work, his readers will find much to learn, much to ponder, and much to admire. Here again, the emotional journey of his poetry will be conveyed most fully to those who can listen with the inner ear and open their minds to the thoughts and images that will resonate most deeply in the oral recitation of these poems.

For this reason, it is entirely fitting that Hawkins has received an endorsement from Phil Myatt, the internationally renowned promoter of 'Mothers – The Home of Good Sounds', and particularly fitting that Myatt regarded Hawkins as worthy of being named the House Poet of this famous rock club. Although Hawkins never did manage to read his poetry at 'Mothers' between sets by Pink Floyd and Led Zeppelin, one certainly imagines that he would have risen to the challenge of doing so! His poetry is strong enough, and his voice sufficiently robust, to stand on its own amid performances by the mythic titans of rock and roll.

And so (in the words of Led Zeppelin) 'as we wind on down the road, / Our shadows taller than our souls', let us keep an eye out for readings and recitations by Russell Hawkins. Like the traveling bards of ancient times, he may be coming to a mead hall near you, and you should go see him recite his poems. You will hear words of great magic and mystery, written from the heart and performed with astonishing verve and lucidity. Until then, you have this book.

ABOUT THE AUTHOR OF THIS 'FOREWORD'

James McKusick is Professor of English at the University of Montana and Dean of The Davidson Honors College. He is the author of *Coleridge's Philosophy of Language* (1986) and *Green Writing: Romanticism and Ecology* (2000). He is the co-editor of *Faustus: from the German of Goethe*, translated by Samuel Taylor Coleridge (2007).

Contents

Note from the Author

Dear Reader,

It is with you in mind that this has been written, and as with any author it is my sincere hope that you enjoy this book. However, if any of the views or opinions expressed conflict with your own, please try to see them as a counterpoint from which ideas, beliefs and understanding may further evolve. As Voltaire said:

"I may disapprove of what you have to say, but I will fight to the death for your right to say it."

As an ex-military officer, martial artist etc, it has raised more than one eyebrow that I have confessed to being a poet. With opinions ranging from one extreme to the other, it has proved to be an *interesting* journey. Yet it is thanks to those who have been encouraging that I owe a huge debt of gratitude. Any of you who have the desire to express yourself in art, just do it and ignore the naysayers - and there are plenty of those. The lesson they have taught is that poetry - in our modern society - is something only for the brave, resilient and thick-skinned.

So what is poetry? Poetry is an art that predates written prose by thousands of years. Rhythm, rhyme and metre have been used by the elders of societies to instruct and entertain for centuries - well before Chinese characters or Egyptian hieroglyphics. It is with this in mind that I try to write, so that it may be read out or performed. Not that much of this is ever likely to be heard by an audience, I still like to respect our collective tribal traditions.

Poetry is also a flow, an adventure, a package of meaning, of words making music... it is life. Life expressed and brought to fullness within ourselves; from our soul, heart, mind, intellect, emotions and our raw physical self. Poetry plumbs the heights, breadth and depth of human experience; poetry speaks to our "aliveness", interaction and at-one-ment with creation. Poetry justifies our right to *Be* as we witness, record and reflect the marvels, miracles and mayhem of the world around us. For it is by this most precious and natural medium that we can truly know another's heart, mind and soul. This, dear reader, is why I believe poetry is Life and Life is Poetry, for they are a mirror of the other - now, ever and always.

With much love - for you are all a living wonder, miracle and jewel of creation.

When reading the poems on the Divine, feel free to substitute the word God for whichever name you feel most comfortable with which refers to the "Prime Mover". He is known by many different names in varying religions or "systems". A few such examples are as follows: Allah, Jah, Jehovah, The Absolute, The Creator, The Force, The Great Architect, The Oneness, The Supreme, The Tao, The Universe and Universal Mind - to name but a few.

I Would like...

I have a poem I would like to write,
That's deep, meaningful and full of insight.
Yet with this pen, which I know works well,
Can I write such a tale that a message will tell?

Of: The Dragons of the Wind,
Or horses by a river,
Or swans on the wing,
Or a Tonka Toy Digger!

But in all of the time
I have yet to live
This one small gift
I would like to give.

A story of depth,
A rhyme of meaning,
A poem of breadth,
A legend revealing!

Of the lives we lead,
Like a process unveiling,
Like watching a seed
As it's germinating.

I would write about life,
In such glorious detail,
About warfare and wives,
But I'm scared I would fail...

To convey the wonder,
The awe and the why,
Of this cosmos alight,
Until the day that I die!

Val d'Isere
15th of March 2004

God – Who Sees and Hears All

God the Seer,
He sees all that has been,
and all that will be
and all that there is across Eternity.
From the time before Time,
when He stirred the Sea
of Nothingness from which arose all galaxies
and all universes across Infinity.

He sees everything in Time
until after Judgement Day
and all that happens in every way.
He has given sight to us in his creation,
phenomenal yet limited in its perception.
We see only objects in a limited space,
unable to see beyond this confined place.
Our sight is limited and we cannot see Him,
yet He sees what we do and what goes on within
our hearts and our minds in every detail,
and if we follow His Prophets we will never fail
to please our creator and never sin,
and he who sees and knows himself
knows that God sees him.

So to know life beyond Life,
eternal Heavenly bliss,
is simply to know we're a creation of His.
When you stand before a brother
can he see into your heart?
This one who is another,
distinct and apart.
He cannot know your motives or needs,
so judges you only by your outer deeds.

Yet God who created you and all before,
He who protects you, sustains you,
Loves you and more,
gives you all that you have,
or could ever wish for;
Yes, our Creator,
The One I Adore.

He who is without and within you
by night and by day;
He is closer to you
than your jugular vein;
He who feels all your pleasure,
and all your Pain...

Every moment of your life know He can See;
this one you depend on for Eternity;
yet in front of His eyes without fear or respect
do you tell lies or His teachings reject?
Is it because you cannot see Him
that you believe God The All Seeing can't see you sin?

(All Hearing)

He is the One who hears all things,
the thoughts of our minds,
the grasshopper that sings,
the beating of all butterflies wings,
the rustle of leaves blown by the wind.

He hears the growing of plants,
the footsteps of ants,
the scuff of the dancers' feet as they dance,
the meteors and comets hurtling through space,
and what's felt in the hearts of the whole human race;
the accelerations of atoms as they move through the void,
and He definitely hears when one is destroyed!

He hears every voice, in every tongue,
and the voice of our conscience when we're doing wrong.
All things heard each as clear as the other.
There's a reason for this, my sister, my brother;
all is registered, responded to and understood,
the guilty are punished,
He rewards the good;
and when a soul to heaven does cry,
the call is heard and then satisfied.

He hears All without distraction.
Those with ears to hear,
show an attribute of His perfection.
There are none like Him in this manifestation.
Any who seem so are just a reflection,
a means, a method, a path to understand,
His Truth in creation,
a guide for salvation,
One we can walk with in peace hand-in-hand.

Those who truly See and those who truly Hear,
Are those to whom God draws near.
They become the eyes He sees with,
the ears with which He hears,
becoming more loving and wise as they grow in years.

Birmingham
June 2008

Mind

A universe of creation,
This is the human mind!
Dare we delve within it
To see what we will find?

There beneath the surface
A mystery to know!
A rhyme, a verse, a story,
Who can say just what will flow?

When the mind is open,
Like a flower it is fed,
Open to creation
That is the mind well read.

Absorbing information
From every human creed,
All experience is education,
Each idea is a seed.

A seed which brings salvation may also bring damnation!
Which ideas to indulge and which to leave behind?
Born in this colossal, crucible of creation,
That is the living miracle of our thinking human mind!

Kidderminster
July 2003

The Way We Go

A trillion paths to choose from,
To walk in infinite manner,
An awareness to select our route,
We are all our own lives planner.

Choices made from knowledge learned
As we have walked our way.
Knowledge learned with Time's passage
Through choices taken yesterday.

Each decision based on what's gone before,
Then blended with our nature.
The free will to choose, who could ask for more?
Life is our greatest teacher.

Hindsight is a blessing
We can look back and reflect,
To ponder, learn and know,
The best path to select.

So when in reflection, you question,
Why you have gone your way.
Just know you chose as best you could,
Each day, by day, by day.

Kidderminster
August 2003

Dancing Like a Moonbeam

Dancing like a moonbeam,
all energy and flair;
a host of blessings on her,
from toes to tips of hair.

A reflection of the Sun;
the nature of life's flow;
from season unto season
her loveliness will grow.

With love and understanding,
she will grow and come to know,
the gold in each brief happening
as she passes through Time's flow.

Dancing like a moonbeam,
with sparkles in her hair,
a universe flows through her,
dare we stop to care?

Care about her passing,
a ribbon of memory,
of God's part in this play,
that flows through such as we.

We upon the stage,
to do just as we will.
From purest bliss to blackest rage,
to love, or to kill.

Knowing Heaven, knowing Hell
is but our choice to make.
The ranks of Hell do swell,
when another's life one takes.

Dancing like a moonbeam,
all energy and flair,
a host of blessings on her
until a bullet parts her hair.

Her memory now distant,
as days flow on and on,
but God displays this instance,
at our Judgement Day's swansong.

"I was only obeying orders."
Never, ever counts.
It's your choice and your will
that's what life is all about.

Without a Judgement Day,
Creation is a joke.
So let's pray to go the loving way,
and help each other out.

Dancing like a moonbeam,
a revelation in the air,
of beauty through times passing,
let her never have a care,
or bother 'bout the bullet
she will never see,
a life of perfect happiness,
like the one you'd love your life to be.

Dancing like a moonbeam
until her hundredth love filled year,
at peace and so serene,
shedding only loves sweet tears.

Birmingham
July 2008

Candle Meditation

There's a lady from a dream,
whom I had flown away,
subtle and serene,
a heart of perfect day.
The Sun shining within her,
a star blazing bright,
a beacon burning brightly,
to these worlds of light and night.
She shines within a flicker,
a tantalising leap,
the space within the flame,
the form which she now keeps.
She tends each loving flame,
she flows within the light.
She burns a path within me
to the Loving Heart of Life.

The glory of her keeping,
that great and peaceful flow,
to connect the heart
and so now part,
the Veil so we may know;
know her for a messenger,
a dear and loving guide;
just see the flame within the flame,
and then enjoy the ride.
The ride through the mind,
upon the candle light,
to the place of peace we find,
when the Will exerts its might.

Birmingham
10th of August 2006

Snowfall

Snowflake petals falling through the mist,
The careworn Earth radiant as she's kissed,
Covered in Heaven's Glory; she's softly caressed,
As by a tender sky she's purely dressed.

*This poem was written on a perfectly still day, with cloud
down to ground level as large clumps of snowflakes fell
vertically out of the sky, covering the ground within a matter
of minutes. It was during the month of April and it had been
very hot prior to the cold front that had arrived. Outside the
kitchen window was a large cherry tree in full blossom and it
was a rare sight to see the Earth covered in a thick blanket of
virgin snow....*

Courchevel
April 2005

Kubla Khan (Or, A Vision in a Dream) (*A Fragment*)
– With a Suggested Ending

In Xanadu did Kubla Khan
A stately pleasure-dome decree:
Where Alph, the sacred river, ran
Through caverns measureless to man
Down to a sunless sea.
So twice five miles of fertile ground
With walls and towers were girdled round:
And here were gardens bright with sinuous rills,
Where blossomed many an incense-bearing tree;
And here were forests ancient as the hills,
Enfolding sunny spots of greenery.

But oh! that deep romantic chasm which slanted
Down the green hill athwart a cedern cover!
A savage place! as holy and enchanted
As 'ere beneath a waning moon was haunted
By woman wailing for her demon lover!
And from the chasm, with ceaseless turmoil seething,
As if this earth in fast thick pants were breathing,

A mighty fountain momently was forced:
Amid whose swift half-intermittent burst
Huge fragments vaulted like rebounding hail,
Or chaffy grain beneath the threshers flail;
And 'mid these dancing rocks at once, and ever
It flung up momently the sacred river.
Five miles meandering with a mazy motion
Through wood and dale the sacred river ran,
Then reached the caverns measureless to man,
And sank in tumult to a lifeless ocean:
And 'mid this tumult Kubla heard from far
Ancestral voices prophesying war!

The shadow of the dome of pleasure
Floated midway on the waves;
Where was heard the mingled measure
From the fountain and the caves.
It was a miracle of rare device,
A sunny pleasure-dome with caves of ice!

A damsel with a dulcimer
In a vision once I saw:
It was an Abyssinian maid,
And on her dulcimer she played,
Singing of Mount Abora.
Could I revive within me
Her Symphony and song,
To such a deep delight 'twould win me,
That with music loud and long,
I would build that dome in air,
That sunny dome! those caves of ice!
And all who heard should see them there,
And all should cry, Beware! Beware!
His flashing eyes, his floating hair!
Weave a circle round him thrice,
And close your eyes with holy dread,
For he on honey-dew hath fed,
And drunk the milk of Paradise.

Samuel Taylor Coleridge, 1797

Kubla Khan Completed
– A Suggested Ending by R.L. Hawkins

Oh maid, oh maid what was your song?
Mind mine do tell me so.
For in this moment is my need,
Your symphony to know.
You sang of love,
You sang of peace,
Your song did touch my heart,
Of the joy of grace and purity, of Love that ne'er departs.
Your song of reason, rhyme and skill,
I do seek to know,
My ignorance I must kill,
My heart and soul to grow.
She sang a song of Mount Abora
From where Alph the sacred river flows
And I to meet, her rhyme a riddle,
Then in my heart, deep in the middle,
There I heard her song.
Within each heartbeat she has called me,
Each heartbeat loud and long.
In silent meditation her face I clearly see.

Beyond the grave, her whispers sweet,
She opens up a door;
There in my heart, behind each beat,
Beyond the fires of passions heat,
Lies the place where we will meet,
The one whom I adore.
So I set to work to live within her score,
To listen to her love divine,
Her love untold, her love sublime,
Until her love is truly mine,
This is what I fight for.
Beyond the grasp of flesh and bone,
Beyond the dirt of earth,
Lies a place that I call home,
A place where All may freely roam
But just what is this worth?
She is a love beyond all telling,
Mere words cannot describe
The joy, the happiness in my being
And in my heart does now abide.

So now I walk up Mount Abora
Within its darkest core;
I entered via the sacred river
Against the river's flow,
For deep within I heard a whisper
This was the way to go.
Three paths to choose to the peak;
One direct, but oh so steep,
One a spiral for the meek,
One dark as pitch, an abyss so deep,
This, my way through Abora's Keep.
Into my heart I did bore,
To know the maiden's heavenly score
That tells of love divine.
And, then, did I reach
Mount Abora's heady peak,
Where the light does purely shine.
I held this light within my eyes,
Reborn that I may never die.
For night was day and day was night,
For Love and Truth I do fight,
I am the loving life of Light
And the living breath of Death.
Yet now, in truth, I sigh,
For words may not describe,
So I will allude to this Love,
Whom All may know in Time.

And so I built that dome in air,
By the River Alph so fair,
And all did cry, Beware! Beware!
His flashing eyes, his floating hair!
They all wove a circle 'round me thrice,
And closed their eyes with holy dread,
For on honeydew they saw I'd fed,
And my light they did despise,
For I'd drunk the milk of Paradise,
So from me they now fled.

Yet as the years passed,
Each of them did sadly die,
Till now none were left to know
How I gained my flashing eyes.
Down the River Alph they swarmed
To dance upon its might,
Each twist and turn made them yearn
For caverns of darkest night.
On and on and on they went,
Till all their precious life was spent,
For from their hearts song they had fled,
Now they were doomed, and they were dead.

Then I heard a wailing cry,
And with floating hair and flashing eyes,
A woman of pure heart, yet doomed to die,
In meditation I did spy.
So I let her see my light,
To give her the will and strength for flight.

(Kidderminster, 20th of June 2004)

So now, you will surely see
Why I did a pleasure dome decree.
This woman below the Cedern cover,
And of the Sunless Sea,
Didst this spark of light now spy,
From my bright and flashing eyes.
She questioned anxiously: *Oh how? Oh why?*
And as she wailed for her demon lover,
A spark within chose to discover,
A way to end her mournful cry.
A way to leave this dreadful plight,
To see my light and make all aright.

And so the pain of time to ply,
Abandoning the dark,
She fought her fight against the river;
The Dome she made her mark.
She cried and wailed against the spate,
Her demon called out songs of hate
Through caverns in the dark.
Yet she made her heart decide
– And conquering her lust –
True love hath she
For the light she did see
In the cavern of the Sunless Sea,
And gain that light she must.
Against the maelstrom did she ride,
The sacred River Alph she plied,
For she to stand by my side,
Or be ground into dust.
And the ancestral voices raised their score
And called out boldly songs of war
To aid her in her fight.
Against the River Alph, she roared for victory this night.

Then gently teasing warm seduction from her demon lover,
Came and rolled around her from the cavern cover:
  Come back to me and cease your flight,
  I'll give you naught but love this night.
A thrill to hear his words so dear,
Heard with more than just her ears,
And her trembling thighs.
Such sweet sensations now caress
Her lovelorn lips and heaving breast,
All to end in sighs.
  What of the light of his eye?
  Her heart did now boldly cry.
  Wondering: *Oh how? Oh why?*
  How to behold that Knight?
  Also the ancestral score
  Which prophesised this holy war
  To find my Lord of Light.
  Against this river I have fought,
  Tell me that it's not for naught
  That I did endure this fight.

Yet my demon lover seduces me
With the sweet sensation of his harmony,
But slowly killing me is he,
In the realm of the Sunless Sea,
Where I wail, cry and die.
And though his song is of love
These feelings are a lie,
The light within comes from above
Where I must return or die.
I will fight on against the Alph,
Against the demon song,
And go to where my heart doth guide
For it's where I do belong.

With a will of iron she made her choice,
Though the way was cruel and long.
For she escaped the demon's voice,
Her heart proved pure and strong.
So as her Khan, I did decree
That she should hear my Symphony,
Which made glory of her Fight and Sacrifice.
To live in light and love of heart,
All her vice she did depart.
For I know the power of her demon lover
And all the spells he tells,
It's what caused us to live apart,
That fractured the love of our heart,
And plunged us into Hell.

So I sang a song to lend her strength against the raging river.
My words she heard and perceived
That I had strengthened her in deed.
To the right! I commanded her,
Then the water split apart,
And she and I at once were joined
By the love within our hearts.
A gentle stroll upon the bed
Of stone so long worn down,
But to the left if she did go
She would so surely drown.

And there, where Xanadu did stand,
In all the worlds of time,
The union of divided love, united so sublime.
By the caves of ice she stood,
Clothed in love and light and blood,
Where she beheld my eyes of flashing light,
No mere mortal man,
For she'd succeeded in her fight
And to me she now ran.
She did not have a care
Of my flashing eyes, my floating hair,
Nor weave a circle round me thrice,
Nor close her eyes with holy dread,
For she too on honeydew hath fed,
And drunk the milk of Paradise.

And this is why, in Xanadu, I did decree,
By where Alph the sacred river, runs to that sunless sea,
My stately pleasure dome,
My Joy that she is home,
A place for her who lives…*Eternally*.

(Kidderminster, 5th of November 2003)

Kubla Khan Completed – Epilogue

And how did she come by this prize
Of her own floating hair and flashing eyes?
By cutting through the demon's lies
And seeing through his fair disguise.

From sunless sea to caves of ice,
Slaying all her Earthly vice,
And drinking the milk of Paradise.
Until she arrived to be
  – here with me,
Living 'ere eternally.
From Death's coil she is now free,
By pain,
  – and will,
    – and bravery,
Her courage plain
  – for all
    – to see.

The prize sublime,
– Love Divine –
For conqueror of space and time.
She solved the riddle of my rhymes.
And now she shines with her own Light –
A candle flame now alight,
From the spark she once did spy,
From my bright
   – and flashing eyes.

The path was trod
And battle won,
She fought her fight on and on,
Against the Alph's mighty spate,
Demons wrath, lies and hate.
Her Holy War is now complete,
At last she takes her rightful seat,
And as the sunless sea retreats,
She and I, at last we meet,
Creation's greatest, loving feat.

Eternally free,
Is she,
Now here with me,
The Reward… Joyous *Immortality*.

Birmingham
22nd of April 2009

The above is a suggested ending to the famous unfinished work Kubla Khan (Or, A Vision in a Dream) by Samuel Taylor Coleridge, who composed the poem in a dream. This conclusion to Kubla Khan has the full approval of the Right Honourable the Lord William Coleridge – Chairman of the Friends of Coleridge academic group – et al.

Samuel Taylor Coleridge wrote the poem at the age of 29 and stated that the work should have been between 200 to 300 lines long. Unfortunately he was disturbed prior to completing it by "the man from Porlock", who kept him busy for two hours. When Coleridge returned to his desk he was unable to finish the poem as he had forgotten it. The Bard attempted to complete the work over the remaining years of his lifetime but was unable, and for the past 200 years it had remained unfinished. This ending weaves a story solely from the original 54 lines and covers all aspects mentioned, without introducing any new characters or subject matter, merely expanding upon the scene as set by Samuel Taylor Coleridge.

The conclusion to the poem has developed over three stages; resulting in an added 246 lines; thus leading to a total of 300 lines in all.

The completed work can be viewed from several perspectives:

1. It is a love story and an ending to a famous poem; nothing more.

2. From the author's perspective it is useful for the reader to view it with the following points in mind:

a) That it is a spiritual odyssey describing the soul and personality's subsequent reunion with the divine.

b) God the Creator of all came first; therefore He is masculine. The soul is a creation of the Creator, therefore in its relationship to the Creator it is feminine. However, the soul is masculine in relation to the body because the soul was created first, and it is the body that is feminine in relation to the soul regardless of gender. Finally, the personality is something that evolves over time through us experiencing life in a body. The body – *in this instance* – is therefore masculine, regardless of gender, in relation to the evolving and refining personality, which is consequently feminine – regardless of personality type.

3. Conclusions from other perspectives can be highly valid. Whilst at the Friends of Coleridge academic gathering in 2006, one of the academics ventured an opinion on what the poem's ending was about. From that perspective his deduction was accurate. However, the perspective that the author had written it from was quite different. That said, the academic was still correct as a valid conclusion from any perspective is still useful.

4. Any further clarification would be like eating a piece of fruit and describing its taste. It is left to the readers to draw their own conclusions and so exercise and nourish their own mind.

Kubla Khan in this complete form describes certain processes and experiences; the essential points of which are summarised in the following poems of 12 lines each...

Union (Or, Every Drop Is the Ocean)

Then I ceased all motion,
And everything did stop,
The drop fell in the Ocean,
And the Ocean in the drop.

Now in infinite splendour,
I gazed into my heart,
Witnessed my creator,
And knew we'd never been apart.

When I broke the stillness,
With but the slightest motion,
The drop fell out The Oneness,
Yet remembered well, The Ocean.

Kidderminster
10 October 2004

From another perspective…

In Silence

In silence and in stillness
My lover comes to me,
And greets me with such loving bliss,
Within this Symphony.

The melody, the harmony,
That flows within the light,
As my love unfolds within this score,
Each and every night.

Beyond the clamour and the din,
As still now as the grave,
Lies deep within my simple heart,
The point where I am saved.

Kidderminster
29th of August 2004

The Ballad of the Dark Ladie (*A Fragment*)
– *With a Suggested Ending*

Narrator:
Beneath yon birch with silver bark,
And boughs so pendulous and fair,
The brook falls scattered down the rock;
And all is mossy there!

And there upon the moss she sits,
The Dark Ladie in silent pain;
The heavy tear is in her eye,
And drops and swells again.

Three times she sends her little page
Up the castled mountain's breast,
If he might find the knight that wears
The Griffin for his crest.

The sun was sloping down the sky,
And she had lingered there all day,
Counting moments, dreaming fears-

Dark Lady:
Oh wherefore can he stay?

Narrator:

She hears a rustling o're the brook,
She sees far-off a swinging bough!

Dark Lady:

'Tis He! 'Tis my betrothed knight!
Lord Falkland, it is Thou!

Narrator:

She springs, she clasps him round the neck,
She sobs a thousand hopes and fears,
Her kisses glowing on his cheeks.
She quenches with her tears.

*   *   *

Dark Lady:

My friends with rude ungentle words
They scoff and bid me fly to thee!
Oh give me shelter in thy breast!
Oh shield and shelter me!

My Henry, I have given thee much,
I gave what I can ne'er recall,
I gave my heart, I gave my peace,
O Heaven! I gave thee all.

Narrator:
The knight made answer to the maid,
While to his heart he held her hand,

Lord Falkland:
Nine castles hath my noble sire,
None statelier in the land.

The fairest one shall be my love's,
The fairest castle of the nine!
Wait only till the stars peep out,
The fairest shall be thine:

Wait only till the hand of eve
Hath wholly closed yon western bars,
And through the dark we two will steal
Beneath the twinkling stars! –

Dark Lady: *(Quite demented)*
The dark? The dark? No! Not the dark?
The twinkling stars? How, Henry? How?
Oh God! 'Twas in the eye of noon
He pledged his sacred vow!

And in the eye of noon my love.
Shall lead me from my mother's door,
Sweet boys and girls all clothed in white
Strewing flowers before:

But first the nodding minstrels go
With music meet for lordly bowers,
The children next in snow-white vests,
Strewing buds and flowers!

And then my love and I shall pace,
My jet black hair in pearly braids,
Between our comely bachelors
And blushing bridal maids.

Samuel Taylor Coleridge

The Ballad of the Dark Ladie – Part Two
– A Suggested Ending by R.L. Hawkins

Dark Lady:
And who shall we invite my love?

Lord Falkland:
Oh, all up on our side.
And we'll be protected by God above,
From the Camelot Knights we can't abide!

Thence to war to take what's ours
And wend our way anew,
We'll leave their corpses strewn like these flowers,
Their heads... I dedicate to you!

Dark Lady:

My noble knight! My saviour!
Wouldst thou do all this for me?
Such bold, gallant behaviour!
Such slaughter I would love to see!

Lord Falkland:

Then our honeymoon will be the battlefield.
And a charnel ground our bed;
And in the night to me you'll yield
For then, we shall be wed.

Dark Lady:

Oh, the night, the night of darkest pitch,
Beneath those twinkling stars,
I'll be yours from Queen to Witch,
You'll be my mighty Mars!

Lord Falkland:

And when this war is won,
It will be well understood,
The land will know we've just begun
Our reign of pain… and blood.

A crucifixion we will make
Of Arthur and his Knights,
And to the dungeon we will take
All those as does seem… right.

<u>Dark Lady:</u>
My love, my love, I now confess
Your thoughts are one with mine,
I did at first live in distress,
Now I see God's plan divine.

That we should sit upon the throne,
Ruling over all this land,
Owning all as if our home,
To govern with an iron hand.

Lord Falkland, my beloved betrothed,
With a Griffin on your chest.
Like a mighty hero from days of old,
You soothe my aching breast.

Your strength and valour as a knight,
Are known throughout the land,
You shine in my heart, pure and bright,
And all shall kiss thy hand...

<u>Lord Falkland:</u>
Then on the wedding day we'll march,
Our troops will conquer all.
No mercy shown to man, nor larch,
We`ll burn corpses at our Ball.

Dark Lady:

My love, my love you are like the sun,
Let's seal it with a kiss,
Our wedding day will be such fun,
A pure, unending bliss.

I will cast such spells to dull their minds,
Then they will fly away,
Or stand and fight, to stand and die,
On our fine wedding day.

Lord Falkland:

With my iron troops, your beauteous beguile,
We will ne'er have cause to fear,
For we will sit and smile and chat a while,
As the battle rages near.

Dark Lady:

My love, my love such gifts you give
To delight my gentle senses,
And I do swoon, so glad to live,
In your sturdy strong defences.

Lord Falkland:

Tomorrow is our wedding day
Now let us both retire,
A victory come what may,
Is not my one desire.

Dark Lady:

My love, my love then let us know
Just where our love may lead,
Let us but one night of love
Our wedding day precede.

x   x   x

Narrator:

The bridal throng was gathered,
In the little church so rare
And all were there who mattered,
The rich… the list ends there.

And when the wedding vow was took,
Where any man may say his peace,
The doors – like thunder – crashed and shook,
There stood the Guardian of the Peace.

Three red bands upon his chest,
Three upon his shield,

Knight of Heaven:

'Tis time dearly beloved and blessed,
To Arthur ye shall yield!

Lord Falkland:
Never!

Narrator:
Cried the traitor Lord.

Lord Falkland:
My army will cut you down!

Knight of Heaven:
I'm so sorry, Lord Falkland,
But there's ne'er a soul around.

And since this bed of traitors,
Wouldst turn our fair land into Hell
And thou wouldst wed this dark witch,
Who casts such vile spells,

My blade is drawn, I do not jest,
I see no cause to hold.

Wedding Guest:
I know you!

Narrator:
Cried a wedding guest.

Wedding Guest:
You're Lancelot the bold!

<u>Narrator:</u>
The slaughter visited in that dark Chapel,
With its cross oddly turned around,
So swift and sure of ethereal force,
Yet not was heard a sound.

A master in the Dance of Death!
The streak of lightning bold and true!
He sliced and thrust and danced his dance
As if their every move he knew.

For he The Knight of Heaven, sent
To tame the darkest hearts,
With thrust and bludgeon he now rent,
Their skulls and private parts.

The wedding guests were now attired
In each other's gore,
True Justice for those who conspired
To kill and go to war!

<u>Lord Falkland:</u>
I yield, I yield Sir Lancelot!
Oh, save me from this whore,
'Twas she who beguiled and seduced me so,
To kill and go to war.

Lancelot:
Nay Lord Falkland, I see the signs,
Of this unholy place.
To indulge in sin then blame her so,
Is thine ultimate disgrace.

Lord Falkland:
Then let us joust upon the meadow,
By the babbling brook,
And we will sport as two fine fellows,
Now *please* do take a look!

Lancelot:
I see you clad in armour, Sir,
As if to go to war,
You betray your purpose here,
You and your so-called whore!

And to the horse, you think me mad?
To give you chance to ride!
I'll do no such you vile cad!
You must think my brain has died!

Lord Falkland:
Then the sword it is, and in this place
Where darkness is so strong,
You'll see how weak you are good knight!
Also so truly wrong.

Narrator:

And in a flash the deed was done.
Three bands e'er fared best.
The duel was so clearly won,
By three bands upon the chest.

A lightning strike too fast to see,
Aimed not at hand or heart,
The extremity of the injury,
When body and head depart.

Lancelot:

And you my lady, whom he called whore,
To save his evil skin,
To accuse you so, to start a war,
He confessed your mortal sin!

Yet in this place ye chose his hand,
A church to vice and dark!
There is none blacker in the land!
Ye carry Satan's Mark!

So on your way, you great harlot,
For now we go to see,
The Good King Arthur, at Camelot,
Who will pass judgement over thee.

Narrator:

And so the legend had begun,
In a place where blood flowed hot,
The story of the bold, the brave, the Dangerous,
The Good Sir Lancelot!!!

Val d'Isere
March 2004

The Ballad of the Dark Ladie – Part Three

Narrator:

And the dark Lady
Whom he saved that day,
Was that disciple of darkness,
Morgana le Fay!

And from a little glade,
Well hidden yet near,
Had watched the most beguiling maid,
The bewitching, beautiful, Guinevere.

And as Lancelot led the witch away
She said:

Morgana:
This day he'll rue,
She will destroy him come what may.

Her words sounded so true.

Morgana:
She will beat him from behind,
Get through his every guard,
Invade his very mind,
So predict the picture cards.

Against her might
His will is naught!
She makes no fight
Yet war is fought!

For against her charm
Against her weakness
You will be disarmed
You will be defenceless!

All of this
Shall come true,
Beware the watcher,
So near to you!

Narrator:
For Lancelot did not see,
Of his watcher, had no idea,
And he thought his challenge Morgana
Not the lovely Guinevere.

And so Morgana cast a spell
At the two standing so near,
With words too magical to tell
But with meaning cold and clear.

Morgana:
That these two fools shall fall in love
And be known throughout the land,
That Camelot shall fall from high above
By their very own good hands.

Narrator:
And so the witch proved Falkland true;
It was then that Lancelot knew;
That this dark witch was the one who,
would a peaceful nation slay
To sanctify her wedding day.

Guinevere espied it all
And was most impressed;
But when Morgana she now saw
She became quite distressed.

For Morgana was a witch of power,
None greater in the land.
Guinevere had studied in her tower
But to light she turned her hand.

And when Morgana cast her charm,
Guinevere could perceive,
That all would surely come to harm
If the magic did succeed.

So with a sign and word or two,
She broke from her good cover.

Guinevere:
I take it you know what you do?

Narrator:
Questioned Arthur's queen and lover.

The force of spell no man can tell,
For in that moment light and dark,
A magic so severe was cast,
It seemed Morgana hit her mark.

Lancelot:
My Queen, my Queen
By God above!
Let me tell you
Of my love!...

I love you as the stars love the night,
I love you as the rose loves the light,

I'll love you through the joy and tears,
I'll love you for all our years.

I'll love you with each passing breath,
I'll love you to our very death.

I'll love you through all pain and sorrow,
I'll love you for all tomorrow,

I'll love you as day loves night and night loves day,
I'll love you with all I do and say.

I'll love you as night loves day and day loves night,
I am loving you with all my might.

I see the light of love this day,
Stay and listen, heed what I say!
Do not turn and run away,
I shall now speak, come what may.

Guinevere:
Nay Lancelot hold your tongue!
This witch has charmed you true,
The love you feel is oh so wrong,
Her magic now has you!

Lancelot:
No my queen I am as ever,
Her spell was just a token,
I tell you that my heart speaks true,
The magic is quite broken.

Guinevere:
Can this be real?
Can such be true?
That dire Morgana's spell
Hasn't affected you?

But where then has the magic gone?
I see no place for it to be.
It must have escaped everyone,
For there is no change in you or me.

Narrator:
And there by the babbling brook,
All was deathly silence,
As at Morgana they did look,
Whose face seemed set for violence.

Lancelot:
Speak now witch!
What is wrong!
You evil wretch!
Let's hear your song!

Morgana:
I too love you Guinevere!
With more than heart or mind,
Do let me stay so close and near,
Oh please do be so kind!

So kind as to let me see your smile,
To allow me in your presence,
You have the most enchanting style,
A beauty without pretence!

So let me tell you of my love,
For you are sent from God above!
To guide us through this troubled time,
To grace us with your light divine!

Oh Guinevere I love you so,
To Camelot please let me go!
My noble brother will be glad this day,
To see his beloved half sister, Morgana le Fay!

Guide me please kind Queen,
Allow me to be known,
As your servant and adviser
And power behind the throne!

For I will swear,
With all I do,
To serve you rightly,
To serve you true!

(Or you will live
To regret the day,
That you foreswore,
Morgana le Fay.)

Guinevere:
Then Morgana if this be so,
To Camelot we all will go,
Before The King – there to know,
Just where your loyalties really flow.

Narrator:

The "happy" trio went their way,
And travelled south for many a day,
In castles royal they did stay,
And just what was said, none can say.

But a pact they did swear,
In word and book and blood,
That each others' secrets they would hold dear,
Or please destroy them wholly God!

All their light and all their love,
No one would ever know.
Such secrets are most surely kept
And from secrets "adventures" grow.

Thus did Witch and the Holy Knight
Join forces hand-in-hand;
When they didst see, that both served,
The King of this good land.

He thinks.

Lancelot:

God must be with us,
We have the devil on our side,
Everyone knows this evil cuss
Is the devil's own true bride!

Let our enemies fear her,
And have fear of us as well.
Then they will avoid all war,
Afraid of her dark power and spells.

As Ambassador she may have use,
We will employ her as a spy.
As King's kin she will suffer no abuse,
And we can prime her full of lies.

Narrator:
Morgana was accepted in
The Court of Camelot;
Where she enchanted her good kin
And fertilised her plots!

Morgana:
Great! I hold a seat of power!
To be Ambassador and spy!
To be given my own...Western Tower!
And be so well paid to lie!

'Twas such a little thing,
Bewitching Arthur with a smile;
Now our son will be King!
Men are so easy to beguile.

Mordred! My hearts one delight!
Guinevere now has so little power.
At least she has her lover knight,
As was arranged one dark night,
As we studied in my tower...

Narrator:

Somehow the fall of Camelot,
Was built upon that fateful day,
When Lancelot didst a wedding stop,
And each guest so cleanly slay.

So yes in all the worlds of time,
In a perfect place called Camelot,
There was had the very best of times,
It was a place where blood flowed hot!

Lancelot didst fall from grace
Through his love for Guinevere
But he saved her from the burning stake,
To adulation far and near!

Then after tragic Camlaan,
When The Table passed away,
Lancelot looked at Guinevere
On a clear and sunny day.

He said:

Lancelot:

I saved you from the burning pyre;
Came to your rescue as I could;
Put to rout those filthy liars;
Did my duty as I should.

Narrator:

Guinevere looked at Lancelot,
Love pouring from her heart,
Her Champion had kept his troth,
Now they never need to part.

Lancelot:

Love is an eternal thing,
That dwells within our hearts,
It takes us to Love – The Lord – our King,
The fount where all joy starts.

And so my love,
Come what may,
There will not be
A wedding day.

To prove you good,
To prove you true,
I will make
A pact with you.

I am your Champion,
I am your Knight,
You are my Queen,
You are my Light.

Guinevere:
But Lancelot I want to be
So much more to you in life,
Oh please do now marry me
So I may be your loving wife!

Lancelot:
No my love, my Queen, my all,
Though I do wish this so,
We must prove you true to one and all,
To a monastery I will go.

Guinevere:
Then I too, to a convent,
For I would love to be
Able to thank God all the time
For sending you to me.

Lancelot:
Each day that I abstain,
I'll ponder the mystery of Love.
My mind and body I will train
In my quest for God above.

Narrator:
For 15 years his vow he kept;
He prayed, worked and read.
Then it looked as if he slept,
As he lay dead in bed.

A host of angels – the monks did say –
Didst come on down to mourn
And carry Lancelot's soul away,
To Heaven he was borne.

With such sworn tales of his death
By monks with naught to gain,
Can any mortal who draws breath
Doubt Lancelot's good name?

And so too of Guinevere,
Whose vows were just the same,
She did stay true to hers I hear
Though many tried to come near,
She never played their game.

Lancelot and Guinevere,
Lovers of the Heart,
I wonder what became of them
When life they did depart?

On to other ventures,
Or in heaven born anew,
Or sent back to rectify,
Any harm they did do?

Who knows what Great Dragon
Lancelot does slay,
As Guinevere watches from her ride,
Each and every day.

Or a couple of space farers
A universe to break,
Leaving suns and galaxies,
Spinning in their wake!

Or just a couple of children,
With wooden swords and dustbin lids,
An innocent pair of little scamps,
Just like the Bisto kids!

*　　　*　　　*

(Morgana's spell backfires but this time Morgana
falls for Lancelot.)

Now let us go back to the brook,
With glade so warm and fair
And we shall take another look,
Where all is mossy there.

The spell has been reflected,
Back to Ms Le Fay,
And it has been directed
In another way.

<u>Morgana:</u>
Oh Lancelot, Oh Lancelot,
This day is yours you won!
The greatest knight of Camelot,
Shining like the morning sun!

The foulest traitor has been killed!
By your brave unflinching might!
And I have never more been thrilled!
You are a marvel in a fight!

And this upon the darkest day,
You have my heart by combat!
The great Sir Falkland ye did slay,
And there will be no comeback.

By trial of combat you have won
The Throne within my heart.
We have just begun, to live as one,
Do swear we'll never part!

<u>Lancelot:</u>
Ah, Morgana your spell has you.
Just how long will it last?
Do you speak your heart open and true,
Or will this charm soon pass?

Morgana:

As Arthur's sister I command,
That you should take my gentle hand
And lead me safely through this land,
For against your strength no man can stand.

Lancelot:

Then I shall lead you Miss Le Fay,
And you have the word of Lancelot,
That no matter what and come what may,
I will bring you safe to Camelot.

Morgana:

Then we ride to my brother's side,
For I do now so swear,
To be true kind and your guide,
I swear this so my dear.

The labyrinth I will guide you through,
Of mind and love and power,
And on this path you may now choose,
What'er you wish my flower.

For others may give you lust,
Or cover you in riches,
Or tempt you with seductive vice,
Or confuse your subtle senses,

But what of lust, a passing whim,
Where a rabbit is by far the king.
And seduction a distraction,
And vice an empty sin.

I can offer you more than all;
Guinevere knows this from my tower;
That I make kingdoms rise and fall;
What I offer you is Power!

Or do you choose another road,
To walk in holy grace?
You're like a hero from days of old,
Strong of arm and fair of face.

So why not let me give to you,
Greatest of all knights,
This Earth as does seem your due,
Champion of a thousand fights!

You could rule this wicked world,
As you venture far afield,
As I guide you through the holy war,
To my guidance ye must yield.

Submit to me
Greatest of knights
And I will be
Your guiding light!

With all the passion and the pain,
I see where you may go.
Such mighty secrets you may gain!
Such knowledge dare you know!

But as your guide from Earth to Stars
Upon this you may bet,
You've Strength of Will greater by far,
Than any I have met!

So my knight now cleave to me,
I offer you a mystery,
Of journeys and of questing
Beyond the mortal coil,
Of action and of besting,
With yourself you'll war and toil!

But, I can also see,
Where your virtue now doth go,
So good knight do come to me
And let your greatness grow!

So God will take you by the hand
And lead you where He will.
To flee is death, so make a stand,
It's Ignorance you must kill!

<u>Lancelot:</u>
Morgana I have heard you sing
And seen thy mortal sin!
To start a war against the King!
Who is thine own good kin!

Such temptation you do lay
Before me on your wedding day,
But I must now gently say,
I love another not far away.

Morgana I must tell you
The depth of my true love,
I love the one so close to you
Who is like the moon above.

Her eyes are like an ocean,
Her hand a charm to hold,
Her smile calms all emotion,
Her heart is purest gold!

Our eyes they met one sunny day,
I knew her 'ere our meeting,
'Twas in the month of June or May,
...I am now quite forgetting.

Her eyes met mine, a sight divine,
Unveiled before my eyes,
But oh so many questions,
So many how's and why's...

We've met before as lovers true
And we will meet again,
And we will know the good from bad,
In the sunshine or the rain.

(Lancelot turns to Guinevere)

Well, as I said, the sun was shining,
And I knew you for the gift you are,
Helper and a friend,
And together we'll go far.

Across the bounds of time we go,
Our love divine God truly knows.
That we together live and grow,
As from day to day we weave and flow.

(Lancelot turns back to Morgana)

My love for her is like the sun
That warms the darkest wood,
And I give my purest love to her
As any true friend should.

Like the moon upon clear nights,
A joy so to be seen,
She is such a loving, living light,
She is perfectly serene.

Narrator:

Who then could this goddess be?
What does his riddle mean?
Then Morgana understood,
He truly loved The Queen.

Alas, alas and woe betide!
Lancelot's Love is clear!
He loves Arthur's Queen, his wife, his bride!
Loves the bewitchingly beautiful Guinevere!

Morgana hatched within her mind,
A plot so mean and cruel,
To behave so sweet, so meek, so kind
And play them all for fools!

<u>Morgana:</u>

So love is love, a sweet riposte,
I see now how things are.
For I too love this metalled ghost,
And now we two will war!

<u>Narrator:</u>

So thence to Camelot they did go,
She pondered in her plotting,
But such a plan no man may know,
Morgana's full of cunning!

And as the years rolled by
With vice beyond all reason
Morgana's heart did truly die,
As she committed her foul treason!

She stole Excalibur's scabbard,
Which warded Arthur from all harm,
The King can now be injured,
For losing this great charm.

A Treasure beyond measure,
So Arthur may now die!
All for her sweet pleasure,
To hear the nation cry.

A prize so magical and rare,
So glibly thrown aside
But done with thought and plans and care,
To hear: "The King has died!!!"

She seduces Arthur with a spell
And takes him to her bed.
This witch, who'll surely burn in hell,
Then bears his son – Mordred!

She plots and plans within her tower,
With allies cold and dark,
Her every word now rings with Power
As Mordred gets his mystic marks!

With ceremonies secret,
She pours her magical might
Upon the head of Mordred,
Who's now lethal in a fight!

He grows in strength beyond his years,
Is great in force of arms,
Is never one for love nor tears,
His mind warped by such charms!

Mordred born of Witch and King!
Of sister and of brother!
Should this be their or his sin?
Or should we blame another?

Skilled beyond his tender age,
A mind of such fine reason,
But slightly prone to fits of rage,
And as we shall see – Treason?!

So the knights did ride away,
Each upon a quest,
To search for where the Grail lay
And pass such stringent tests.

So many knights did come and go
To the Fisher King
And see the Great Procession,
Yet did not ask a thing.

Then it came to Galahad,
Lancelot's Good son,
And by his Heart so Pure
The precious Grail was won.

Galahad, had his life seen
All in one fleet measure,
When he had supped from the Grail
And gained the Greatest Treasure!

And as he saw all things unfold,
In that brief eternal moment,
He passed through the gates of mystery,
His soul purified, resplendent!

From this Earth he then departed,
His soul to heaven did fly,
So many he left broken hearted,
As, he then, did die.

But as he passed away,
He told his loving friends,

Galahad:
Love all you can in every way
For life goes on my friend.

And when you make your journey,
From one realm to another,
Be sure you've been of service
To God's Light there in your brother.

For as I go my way,
I do for all now pray,
That all may too find Heaven,
On their own great dying day.

And to my father Lancelot,
A man of Love and Might,
Tell him in all of history
He will make the greatest Fight!

A battle beyond telling,
Beyond all means of measure,
It is he who will succeed
To give God the greatest pleasure.

Of what I speak is far away,
Beyond all mortal years.
Yet he will go, the way he knows,
The path that all men fear.

Narrator:
And with that Galahad passed away,
To Paradise he ascended.
The "Seat of Peril" now empty lay
As the Grail Quest was ended.

After this time of questing,
The kingdom did grow colder
As Mordred now was besting
Knights more skilled and older.

In swords there is one truth,
There is but one great measure,
Experience not youth
Is by far the keenest treasure.

So how could it now be
That in all of Camelot
The only Knight he could not beat,
Was the Good Sir Lancelot?

So it was that Morgana set
Into action her greatest plan;
To gain the throne for her own
When Mordred turns a man.

So she did employ
– As her plots began –
A bodyguard for her boy,
To execute her plan.

To lie, to cheat, to stop at naught,
To cause such great commotion,
To get The King to question so
The goodly Queen's devotion.

Morgana:
This knight, Sir Lancelot,
Against whom none can stand,
It truly would be better
Were he gone from this good land.

Then set a trap so all is done,
In one well chosen place,
A place to kill both birds as one
With bloodshed and disgrace.

A ploy to lure the two together
After chaos, stress and a grief,
And we will pick our time when they
Are open, calm and weak!

Narrator:
Much was set in motion
There on that dark day;
The process of devotion
To ensuring the decay
Of this happy nation,
With peace throughout the land,
To ensure the Coronation
Of the blackest hearted man!

A trap was set to cover all
Within the good Queen's chamber.
If Guinevere were against the wall
They could be pushed together.

Morgana:
But how to have the two as one
In any brief embrace?
This act must be seen by some
To give us their disgrace.

Then The Queen to trial goes
And Lancelot the same,
And we'll be the witnesses,
For none doubt our good name.

And she then to the burning stake
As adulteress and whore,
Lancelot beheaded – the faithless rake –
Then we can go to war!

Narrator:
The Bodyguard said:

<u>Bodyguard:</u>
But Lancelot the Warrior,
Prince born of royal line,
Must be without his armour
So we'll stay whole and fine!

We insist he be without,
His armour, sword and shield!
For if he is armed or armoured
Then we must flee the field.

And we really do not like that!
It really cramps our style.
But do not worry about it,
That hasn't happened… for a while.

<u>Narrator:</u>
Morgana found it wholly tragic,
Guinevere had studied well,
The Queen could block Morgana's magic,
Every curse, and hex and spell.

So to be rid of Guinevere,
Lancelot must be gone before.
A trap to set the pair together
So The Queen could be called whore!

The day was set, the treason done.
The pair were seen together,
As Lancelot was called from prayers
To inspect The Queen's new chamber.

As champion and bodyguard
Her safety was his duty.
The room designed was sound and fine,
Proving adequate security.

He inspected all the fittings
With the lovely Guinevere,
And none could be suspicious
As the guards stood very near.

The two were pushed as was planned,
But that was where it ended!
Lancelot could clearly see
What these dark armed knights intended!

With foot and fist he poured his wrath
And cleared the doorway through,
He slammed the door, half bolted it,
Then the bolt withdrew!

A knight fell in the opened door,
Then with a crash he knew,
The door was bolted closed behind
And there was nothing he could do!

A moment later he hit the floor,
A crumpled metal mess,
Time for Lancelot to go to war
In the captured armour dressed!

Lancelot could see their plan,
They had so been set up!
Time now to be a man
And beat the bounders up!

Sword, helm and armour,
And Lancelot the man,
Stood filling in the door
And all the guards now ran!

Lancelot made good
This moment of respite,
And sought to tell The King
Something of his plight!

But Mordred and Morgana
Were working hand-in-hand,
And Arthur was delayed
Somewhere in the land.

So Lancelot set out to find
His liege, his lord, his friend
But fate didst now prove unkind,
And they did not meet again.

Morgana's plans
Now weave and flow,
What of Lancelot?
No one knows...

Morgana:
So we will carry on,
Our plans will stay the same
And it will now be done,
We will win this power game!

Narrator:
So to the stake with The Queen,
In a field full of tears,
As all the crowd had hoped to see
Her grow old and wise in years.

Then through the hedgerow slowly came
A horse with bridal bower,
But paid no heed, for the horse was lame,
Although much bedecked with flowers.

An explosion from the horse so fair
Of colour, force and flame,
Flowers scattered everywhere,
Lancelot rides again!

A twisted convolution,
Too complex to be told,
Is how he fought for her salvation
So she too may grow old.

Roses scattered everywhere,
The ground was wet and red,
The Court of Camelot's in despair
As knights lay broken, dying, dead.

With the horse
He moves as one!
As living death,
All lameness gone!

He fights to save Her Majesty
But why no armoured guard?
This has turned into a tragedy
For all who have a heart.

For many knights did fall that day
To Lancelot du Lac,
As to The Queen he fought his way
In his valiant attack!

With will and sword of iron he fights,
To cut through chains of steel!
With one great strike with all his might,
The metal meekly yields!

He pulls her down from burning pyre,
Then shouts aloud in pain,

Lancelot:
Why is our Queen now called a liar?
Why is she in these chains?

For as I stood before you all
At Camelot's Great Table,
I swore The Queen to defend and more,
As much as I was able!

As champion and bodyguard
You are all so lax!
To expect me not to rescue her,
Or at least mount some attack!

How can it now be
That I take such love away?
Away across the sea,
"Hi – Ho, Argent, Away!"

Narrator:
With spur and sword he made good
A valiant escape,
Changed horses in many town and wood –
Took a new shield and new cape.

Unmolested went their trip,
Down to the sparkling sea,
And thereupon they boarded ship,
And sailed to Brittany.

And what of the sad carnage
As they did fly away,
There by the burning pyre
Knights battered, dead and dazed.

Upon this day of Death,
On this day of pain,
The Great Good Knight Sir Gareth,
Too was sadly slain.

There upon the Field of Death,
Gawain did now declare,
As he sobbed and fought for breath,
He would find the fleeing pair.

Gewain:
For his actions on this day
And for this act of murder,
For Gareth's death, du Lac must pay.
Brother has killed brother!

To Brittany he has retired,
We follow on the tide!

Narrator:
Through all the nation Lancelot's admired,
All wished him a safe ride.

But for the death of his good cousin,
A knight of noble bearing,
Sir Gawain can see no reason
To justify this killing.

The Court thence on to Brittany,
For Gawain to have his duel,
For one long week Gawain declared,
du Lac a cruel and stupid fool.

Then in armour, sword and shield,
The two they duely fought,
And Lancelot pleaded with Gawain
That they halt this insane sport.

Gareth's death was hard to bear,
For he had been his friend,
And Lancelot took every care
That he did not Gawain's life end.

But Gawain he would not listen,
To bludgeon, word or blow
As Lancelot gently toyed with him,
Till he did surely know,

That Gawain's intention
Was to kill him in this fight,
For he was under the compulsion
That what he did was right.

So after many hours
And after such great pain,
The two stared at each other,
du Lac spoke to Sir Gawain.

Lancelot:
I too loved Gareth like a son,
This grief gives me such pain!
I wish his death could be undone,
And we were friends again!

For I swear to you,
With all I do,
The Queen is chaste,
The Queen is true!

And what of her betrayers?
To believe their poison rot!
To take the word of vipers
Over Queen and Lancelot!

Narrator:
But in his rage he could not grasp
That he was tired and beat,
Sir Gawain did now collapse,
From exhaustion, wounds and heat.

And this is now the darkest day,
When brother again kills brother,
Gawain to Lancelot did say,

Gawain:
Please forgive me now my brother.

How could I have been so wrong?
To judge you so unjustly!
To believe that vile, lying throng,
Morgana must have charmed me!

So keep The Queen safe this day –
And for many more.
To my king I have to say,
Return to England's shore!

For we've been sore beguiled,
Assaulted from within!
Our nation stands defiled,
By Morgana's schemes and sin!

King Arthur:
Thence to the boats to our return
To see what we may see.

To Lancelot, Arthur smiled, and turned,
Saying:

King Arthur:
– Keep her safe for me!

And soon we will send word,
When all is fair and well,
When Morgana's grip is broken,
To return I will thee tell.

Narrator:
Gawain he died – such sad shame,
For all were once more friends,
Arthur swore to clear Lancelot's name,
Some friendships never end.

Their journey back was fair and fleet
Across the foaming sea,
Until at Camlaan they did meet
An army of their enemies.

But Mordred he was with them,
In armour red as blood,
And he pleaded with King Arthur
That their cause be understood.

So Arthur deigned to hear
What they had to say,
And sat upon his horse
Not very far away.

Saxon Boss:
I too was born a Saxon,
'Cos me mum and dad moved 'ere
But I too am a Briton,
'Cos I too was born 'ere!

This is the land of me birth,
I have not done no crime!
What choice did I have in my land,
Or parents of my line?

But you are Arthur and do rule true,
And we do have respect for you!
And for the Law of Camelot!
Which you do 'ave and we've not got.

By your actions,
You did chase away,
You talk and do
Not talk and say.

And because we have respect for you,
'Cos you talk the talk then do the do,
Then we would one become with you,
'Cos you talk the talk... then do the do...

One big fightin' army
Shelters all the land.
Keeping vigil calmy,
If bad men come around!

King Arthur:
A truce, an alliance?
What joy now to behold!
I have had too much of violence,
It turns my blood so cold.

Saxon Boss:
But you are Big King on Big Island,
And All Saxon Kings give you Big Hand.
You the Big King of great might,
You say kill, they will all fight!

They want to have what you got,
Want Good Kings Law of Camelot!
You give them your solemn word,
And they give you their every sword!

Mordred:
Father you must answer him,
Or you'll cause an infraction,
They want to have you as their king,
You must mix words with action.

King Arthur:
In friendship then let us now look
To clasp these Saxon hands,
And once I have his good hand shook,
All shall be brothers in our lands!

So Mordred, you fine marvel!
To achieve this amazing feat,
In diplomacy you have no rival,
You're just what your country needs.

All of Britain united,
Who could think this thing?
I think that in time Mordred
You will make a splendid king.

Your mother taught you well –
For with this bloodless battle won,
You and I can tell her
That I love you as my son.

Hear this, my fair subjects,
To mark this happy day,
I now empower Mordred
That all do as he says.

For in this happy hour,
On this delightful day,
We will walk and talk as brothers,
As we wend the hours away.

But armies are deadly beasts,
And to ensure good behaviour,
If any man draws his blade,
This Great Alliance is over!

Narrator:

Two mighty armies intertwined,
A great and happy greeting
But like the finest laid of schemes,
No plan survives first meeting.

And all did call each other friend,
Before that bloody lake.
No sooner did the armies blend,
Then a warrior spied a snake!

A flash of steel, the adder dead!
In a breath the deed was done!
The ground just started to get red,
As every blade now drew as one!

There was no chance to halt the death
That erupted in that field,
As every man there who drew breath,
Knew it was death to yield!

Two great friendly armies,
Died that fateful day,
On a day so calm and balmy
Splintered the table lay.

Broken bodies and shattered swords,
That chaos spreads anew!
Such sadness defies all words,
Such grief; now what to do?

For where the slaughtered armies lay,
King Arthur sat down dying,
To Sir Bedivere he did say:
"Into the lake send my sword flying."

Finally that good knight cast
Into the Lake Excalibur,
Above the waters it was held fast,
Then vanished in a blur.

Ne'er was heard a thing,
Nor any ripple seen.
He returned unto The King,
To tell what had just been.

The King, he smiled, and passed away,
With His Table Great,
In bones and flesh it shattered lay,
Destroyed by the hand of fate.

Then after Camlaan
All did say,
The chance of peace
Was killed that day.

The Saxon cause did triumph,
The Celts they sailed away,
They all returned to Brittany,
Or dead in England lay.

Lancelot looked at Guinevere,
One fine and sunny day,
He told her that he loved her,
'Twas in the month of May.

A love beyond all reckoning,
A love beyond all reason,
A love that stays so sure and pure,
Through each and every season.

And she too was heard to say,
In tones now so familiar,
That she loved him come what may,
In a manner very similar.

And so to carry on the game
They walked a path anew,
And took vows that gave such pain
As they did what they did do.

Away then to a holy life,
Of prayer and meditation,
Though not the vows of man and wife,
They proved their great devotion.

The strength of love between them
Means they will never part,
No matter what the distance,
Holding true each other's heart.

A love so true, a love so strong,
So caring and sublime,
This pair have loved and lost so long
Across the Gulf of Time.

But now upon the close of play,
When all now show their cards,
What could any man now say
As they fly amongst the stars?

*   *   *

Epilogue

The characters chat with the audience/reader.

King Arthur:
**And what could I now say to you,
Now these fair days are over?
And what should you or all men do:
Call all men your brother!**

**So let us take our time,
To learn about each other
So of all beings we may say,
Hey father, mother, sister, Brother!**

Saxon Boss:
For in our hearts,
We is same parts.
You is what we too is!
But we 'ave problems with the lingo,
Until Big Bossa knows how,
To speaky speaky wiv your Kingo –
Like better than what I can does now.

And use your heady noggin'
To find what wordy means,
"Camlaan" is Oldspeak for place where is,
"Snake's bustin' at the seams."

King Arthur:
So not a question of if but when,
When sword was drawn on high,
To strike down at the adder, then
Both armies sure to die.

The plan was hatched at Camelot,
There in the Western Tower,
Where Morgana penned and planned her plot
To destroy the seat of power.

She boasted to so many,
In fact some would say all,
That by her skill and her base cunning,
She could make kingdoms rise and fall.

The statement was a fact
But not all truth some mumble,
For Morgana's only skill
Was in making kingdoms tumble.

It's simply what she liked,
None could credit her so bad,
She was universally disliked,
She died lonely, cold and sad.

*   *   *

Narrator:
Now what say you Good Arthur,
To this audience so dear?
You have lived and loved amongst them,
For many a happy year.

King Arthur:
Aye, I see my purpose,
To speak of things of pain,
To have a brief discourse
About what we wish to gain.

So one small thought to take with you,
As you travel home this night,
That war is wasteful through and through,
And both sides can lose a fight.

Me and these noble players
Now did thee adieu,
Please respect your noble neighbours,
And they will respect you.

We wish you all the best,
In everything you do.
Now we leave you to your rest,
Good audience... Thank you.
Adieu, adieu adieu...

Val d'Isere
April 2004

The Pirate and the Paladin

And there at once the vision struck,
The mind erupted broke and shook,
As all of life now did invert,
Twist and break and reconvert,
Into an open-heart felt love.
A blazing, burning light above.
A single shadow now was cast
Upon the thief of ages past.

The thief, the master of illusions dear,
A dancing, prancing buccaneer.
A rogue so loved beyond all pleasure,
As he slowly stole the greatest treasure.
And now the spotlight 'off' is turned
And all do see that rogue who burned;
With passion's fire,
The heart to deceive,
The perfect liar
And all will grieve.

But for the heart blazing like a sun,
A war ended, a battle won,
With but one fine shadow cast,
On the one for whom life will not last.
He fought his fight with cunning guile,
Word and wink and winning smile
Yet with a nod, sent us to our beds,
Where we danced the dance of the dead.

Once a questing knight did stray,
From his realm so far away,
And entered to another place,
Of peace, tranquillity, love and grace;
Where the battles of the realms of Hell,
No longer held that fatal spell;
That leads all men to war and greed;
He saw the purpose and the need
Of the buccaneer to plant and sow,
He saw the pirate and did now know.
Know wherefore and why,
Why men live and why men die.
In silent battle he did rage,
Imprisoned the pirate in a cage

And bound him in chains of Iron Will.
The knight, the pirate sought to kill.
With fury vast and strength untold,
This buccaneer from days of old,
Didst now strike with all his might,
Against the strong, unyielding knight.
He called the Paladin to yield
But that warrior stayed on the field.
Said to the pirate: Come what may,
I will fight you true till Judgement Day.

Then let us fight and do great battle.
The ground did quake, the trees did rattle
And as these two did now war,
The knight proved greater by far.

Then the Judgement Day it came,
For the knight with strength amassed,
Against the buccaneer he proved true
And judgement now was passed.
The battle had not been in vain,
For he saw the light and way Home again.
Now he stands at Heaven's Gate,
From war, his strength now truly great,
Against the slayer of his kind,
The pirate with the demon mind;
Who casts and weaves his magic spell,
Turning heaven into hell.

The knight returns to his kind,
Strong, true and pure of mind.
Yet the pirate in each man does lie,
For each their choice to fight or die.
He has a way to help them now,
Their own salvation they may plough;
But only those who choose to leave,
The demon whom they know not deceives.
Yet these deceptions in each man grow,
Until his name they'll never know…

The knight has but one thing to say,
Of the time before the Judgement Day,
He says his peace and stays no longer:
"If you have the strength,
'The Fight' will make you stronger."

Val d'Isere
February 2004.

The Light of Life

The light of life burns,
A star in the sky.
A heavenly body;
Now I ask myself why?

The moon in its orbit,
Gently revolves.
Changing, unchanging,
A mystery solved.

An ocean of suns,
Silently blinking.
A gift of pure beauty,
Quietly twinkling.

A world condensed
From the death of a star,
Atoms and molecules
Formed from afar.

The bricks of our body
On which we depend,
A glorious cycle,
Without beginning or end?

The wonder of life
From stars above,
Forms into bodies,
Such glory, such love!

This great universe alight,
Upon which we depend,
Giving itself and you life,
Are you its enemy or friend?

To allow itself to be,
To allow yourself to grow,
You're a child of all this,
Don't fight it, just flow.

Go with a heart
At one with the All,
Serve it then yourself
And we'll all have a Ball.

Giving life to each other,
There's so little we need,
It's our great Father-Mother,
Let's abandon our greed.

Mimic Mother Nature,
So good to Herself,
Growing and changing,
From poisons to health.

The cycle of life,
A miracle to witness,
Such perfect equilibrium,
This I have to confess.

So when you look into the sky,
On a day warm and bright,
Just know your life's power
Is contained within the light.

And when you look into the sky,
On a night cool and clear,
The stars that burn brightly
Are ever so near.

Closer than hearing,
Closer than touching,
It's the skin you are wearing,
Your body that's breathing.

The body made of stars,
Both living and dead,
You're a child of the cosmos,
A being well blessed.

You're alive,
You're unique,
You're at one,
You're complete.

All of creation
Is poured into you!
You are precious past measure,
Be Aware what you Do!

The universe laughs as you laugh.
It cries as you cry.
And it reflects on itself,
As you ask yourself: "Why?"

Kidderminster
August 2004

The inspiration for the above poem came after watching a TV programme describing how the universe and we were created.

Originally, after the Big Bang (or for Creationists: The Wonderful Word – both being sounds...), there were only hydrogen atoms in existence. The process of gravity caused hydrogen atoms to be drawn together; eventually through pressure and heat, the nuclear fusion engines started and suns were born. In the heart of the suns, heavier and heavier molecules were formed. Eventually the suns died and left behind a host of heavier elements. Then in our region of space, a load of dust, gas and "dead" stellar material came together due to gravity (or the shock wave of an exploding supernova), and so formed our own solar system.

Through an unfolding process, matter forms into life; this ultimately relies on the Sun for its nourishment, via photosynthesis. The Sun provides energy for the plants, which we then eat and so fuel our bodies and/or consume the animals which feed on the plants. So effectively, we are stellar beings, children of the stars. The atoms of our bodies were forged in the hearts of long dead stars, and the energy that powers them now is ultimately derived from our own yellow sun. Creation is truly magnificent, mesmerising and miraculous.

One...

I think of the time when all is One,
this bittersweet life has simply gone;
yet what we are still echoes on;
an echo hence
   – from whence
     – we've come;
sounding true by what we've done;
as Time
   – and the Divine
     – has born
       – and borne
         – us on --
that precious, priceless echo....
   – From ....
     – anon...

Birmingham
April 2009

I Am...

It is normally considered bad form to introduce a poem with an explanation. However, there is always an exception and I feel this is just such an occasion. To stay with poetic protocol the explanation is at the poem's end but it may prove beneficial to read it first.

I am a Russell on a mountain,
a ripple on a lake,
a sparkle in a fountain,
a tear at a wake,
a halo
like a rainbow
in the mist around the moon,
a star rising in the desert,
a rendezvous at noon,
the power in a heartbeat,
the riddle in a rhyme,
the rythm in my feet,
the flux in Space and Time.
I am the carer
and the slayer
of the love that drives my life,
the mercy and compassion of the universe's light.

The wonder
and the terror
of the heavens and the hells,
the Dragon's primal rider,
the magic in a spell.
The power in a pen point,
the passage of Light's flow,
the strain on a bowstring,
the tension in the bow.
I am the parallax of fortune,
the groominthrond of luck,
and the poet sent to tease you,
with a word I just made up.
I am a universe's child,
supported by a star's good light,
I am a poet and a player,
promoted to shovelling shite.
I am a junction in the nexus,
of the Loving Life of Light,
in the form and flow of Russ,
in this zone of life's twilight.

I am the rhyme within this rhythm,
which you'll love or despise;
the door of truth lies open,
or do you prefer the world of lies?
Have you come to be enlightened?
But do instead now find,
that you've been hypnotised,
by the fractals of your mind?

Love or loathe this rhyme,
it's irrelevant you see,
for we are one in space and time,
and you... are just like... me.

Sonthofen
February 2008

*When we hold a pen, the pen is considered to be an extension
of our person. With that in mind, the paper is also seen to be
an extension, so the table, the chair, the floor and
consequently the surroundings. So too, anything we
experience is an extension of us, and we of it, as we are part
of the collective whole of the experience. This is what was in
mind when writing the above.*

The Tour de France of Lance Armstrong

Men of steel,
Pumping hard,
Are they for real?
As they go far!

Above the crowd,
Men so high!
Rightly proud,
They do or die!

Upon the mountains
They valiantly race,
Power Fountains,
For the Yellow Ace!

The one who battles
Day and night!
Discipline's disciple,
In this ultimate fight!

He is the one,
Who won't be beat,
Indulgence gone,
To win each heat!

Dedicates each living breath,
He is beyond all sinning!
A chocolate bar is seen as death,
Upon his road to winning!

M40 between London and Birmingham
29th of August 2004

For Philip Myatt – Promoter

I'm glad I've known him though our time is passed.
Our flesh is simply not made to last;
once we are born the die is cast;
life is too short and Phil lived fast.

He burnt his candle at both ends;
chopped it in half, then quarters then –
set fire to the new loose ends;
it's a miracle he lived till we were friends.

And best friends, aye,
he and I,
he trained me well, though I wonder why,
I guess we just saw eye to eye,
can I be sad now he's died?

Not a chance;
he danced his dance;
the finest dandy wove and pranced;
yet when confronted made his stance.

Stood like a knight,
took no fright,
seemed like Rommel to the sight
and quite the General in a fight.

And his magic gave us such delight;
all thanks to his great insight;
he backed the winners – proven right –
and wow could he fly a kite!

So old friend,
now at the end,
your wild ways ye did mend,
there's no one can contend –

You're the greatest rock promoter the world has ever seen!
The biggest and best there has ever been!
Whilst others may bluff, preen themselves and dream,
you my friend were the Cream of the Cream.

So much so, the world will know,
that such great talent you let flow,
and then simply let them go,
to shine and glow and still they grow;
such great lights listed below:

**Pink Floyd, Led Zeppelin, Mothers of Invention,
The Moody Blues, Black Sabbath and Fairport
Convention**.

Al Stewart, Audience, Robert Plant,
Taste, The Faces and The Deviants.

Spirit, Santana, Otis Span,
Traffic, T-Rex and Caravan.

Argent, Supertramp, Every Which Way,
Fleetwood Mac, Chicken Shack and Fotheringay,
plus The Strawbs, Savoy Brown and Jan Dukes de Grey.

David Symmonds, Pete Drummond, Action,
Jethro Tull, John Peel and Eclection,
plus Chicago, Skid Row and the Graham Bond Initiation.

Hawkwind, Colosseum, Blossom Toes,
Yes, Swagus and Stone the Crows.

Joe Cocker, Atomic Rooster, Duke Boy Bonner,
Taste, The Nice and Magna Carta.

King Crimson, Retaliation, Saffron,
Deep Purple, The Who and Elton John,

And the list goes on and on and on and on...

A book was written about "Mothers".
The Greatest Club – above all the others,
where all were sisters and loving brothers.
Birmingham City Library commissioned "Mothers –
The Home of Good Sounds". Where the arts did thrive
and Love, Peace and Brotherhood really came alive,
and as a consequence your name will survive,
down through the ages and across the Gulf of Time;
thanks to your insight which was truly quite sublime,
and we have all been blessed that you were once alive.

By The Mothers House Poet
Birmingham
20th Nov 2008

I was introduced to Philip Myatt through a mutual friend.
After hearing my work he wrote a letter and kindly stated that
had I been around at the time of the rock club "Mothers – The
Home of Good Sounds", I would have been the house poet
and had my own corner in the club. Considering that
"Mothers" was voted number one venue in the world by
America's Billboard magazine – ahead of New York and Los
Angeles Philmore East and West, which were considered the
coolest venues in the States at the time – it is a great honour.
Especially when I would have done my performances in the
break between the groups sets....

For Harry Patch "The Last Fighting Tommy"
– My Cosmic Twin (we were both born on the 17th of June)

I wrote this as a complementary response to Andrew Motion –
the poet laureate's work: "The Five Acts of Harry Patch", as
I truly believe that the traditional forms of rhyming poetry
have their place – and I felt that Harry Patch deserved further
accolade in a rhyming format.

> "A curve is a straight line caught bending."
> A little boy in training,
> in the backyard battleground;
> crawling through the cover –
> "dead" if he's discovered,
> he dare not make a sound.
> "The Mission" here survival.
> His parents test his guile,
> as he makes his way around
> to the juicy treasures that abound
> above the entrenched earth
> – potato patch furrows –
> cover beyond worth,
> his battle skills developing with mirth;
> as he mounts a swift attack –
> bites the hanging pears around the back,
> the fruit trees he has sacked.

Truly like a soldier;
Hidden, yet much bolder;
this game, his lifeline when he's older
on those bloody fields of France;
where with Death he danced,
as shrapnel freely pranced;
ripping a boy from waist up to shoulder –
in thirty seconds sixty years older.
His battlefield-brother
who cried no girlfriend's name
at his exit from life's game;
a virgin calling out for "Mother".

Harry's training in the stone mines,
practicing stealth in the dark,
throwing stones at wasps nests,
a young soldier – one apart.
Lying still and silent,
wasps angry, even violent,
escape route has been recced –
a master of his art.
One of many tests
passed by "bad" behaviour
made him a true survivor,
and a soldier in his heart.

Birmingham
Summer 2008

The Sod of War

I fought a war at Gallows Peak,
And crushed an army there.
I burned their corpses for a week,
To fragrance the foul air.

I crossed the plains,
And bore away
the treasures of our age,
Whilst blood and pain
Flowed more each day,
As my ravaged army raged.

I chose the path of bitter tears;
That war and blood should flow.
More out of folly at my few years
To learn what I now know.

That Power is a drug my friend,
and those who know its seed,
Lie broken; weeping at the end,
For their soul sold out to greed.

And when the Reaper came my way,
No Mercy did He show.
What can we say upon the day
Mortality we know?

And as the Veil split apart,
and I stood there boldly,
I felt His Pain deep in my heart
He had no need to scold me.

I did it all to make a name,
So the World would be mine,
Smashed up the board and wrecked the game!
An insult to pigs to call me Swine.

Monger of war was I,
Power was my treasure.
"Buy these guns, have some fun!"
More pain – oh such sweet pleasure $$$

Meribel
April 2005

"Political power comes from the barrel of a gun." – Mao Zedong

Having served in the British military, I have had ample time and reminders of the consequences of going to war. Battlefield injuries are monstrous. (I had plenty of opportunity to study such photographs while serving with an armoured medical unit.)

A well known arms dealer is reported to have boasted that he started wars in order to sell his "products"; and he sold to both sides.

Sir Basil Zaharoff is quoted as stating: *"I made wars so that I could sell arms to both sides," he declared. "I must have sold more arms than anyone else in the world."* – Sunday Chronicle, London, November 29, 1936. Sir Basil is the most famous of all arms dealers (being known as Mr Five Percent), and it was he who epitomised the term *'merchant of death'*. As the chief salesman for Vickers he received £86,000 in 1905 and rapidly became a millionaire. Zaharoff understood the interconnection between arms and power, and all the elements required to "encourage" a population to go to war.

"The sinews of war are infinite money." – Cicero, Roman philosopher and politician

Garden

A Garden of creation,
This is the living Earth.
In all states and nations
All life is giving birth.

You are the children of your land,
The place where you were born.
Raised by your parents' hand,
Are you happy or forlorn?

Do you live in warmth,
Or cold and damp, or frozen?
Is your place upon the Earth
The environment you've chosen?

In the garden that you live in
Can you walk about so freely?
Or are you bound within a box
With bars, hard, grey and steely?

Are you now in torment,
Or a perfect Eden?
Or do you yield on the battlefield?
In this savage garden.

Or do you blaze a trail.
Across the desert sands,
Dive under the ocean,
Or visit other lands?

This garden that we live in
Is ours by choice or reason;
This hothouse of creation
With ever changing seasons.

Val d'Isere
March 2004

Heaven or Hell?

My brothers, my sisters, our planet's a mess.
Our home's a disgrace. Have we failed our test?

Put here on the Earth to do as we will!
And all we do is rape, steal and kill!

A duty of care from the Great God above,
To look after His garden and treat it with love!

Yet look what we've done with this jewel of creation,
Raped it for Greed and caused mass extinction!

Has our stewardship here been a blessing or curse?
Just look what we've done and it's just getting worse!

The waste we produce brings death beyond measure.
We're slaughtering life just to increase our pleasure!

Disease is disease by the poison it passes.
Destroying its host to increase its masses!

The Earth is the host on which we depend.
By destroying Her, it's our own life we end!

So let's clean up our act and treat life with *Respect!*
Stop creating such waste! We are fostering death!

Does Greed now take over? What is this insanity?
We're killing Our home! We're killing Our Humanity!

So let's clean up our act, be a blessing, not a curse,
How many *of God's* species must we put in a hearse?

Let's think with foresight, think of future need!
Let's abandon these systems driven by Greed!

We have got enough wealth.
Let's work on good health.

The health of the planet, which we taste with each breath,
'Cos we're in this together – until we meet Death.

Then, when, it's all finally blown apart
And we are now judged by God's love in our hearts,

When each of us dies, and passes our wake,
The truth and the lies are now ours to partake,

Partake and be measured, by what we have done,
And know if we're treasured, by God who's *The One* –

– Life, Light and Love, so it seems,
He who flows through the night and creates all our dreams.

Has He kept for you a Paradise Place?
Or will you be rejected and deemed a disgrace?

For you will be "rewarded" by what you have done.
Did you care for or enslave it? *Good* Mother's Son?...

Birmingham
11 of July 2006

Mr Big

Mr Big how do you feel?
In your world that's so unreal!
Dealing in your shares and stocks,
Whilst the planet slowly rots.

Profit is your only goal,
This sacred doctrine you uphold,
Living your life by this creed,
Wallowing in your pit of Greed.

You produce nothing, yet have the cream,
Objects of fancy, the workers' dreams.
You have so much yet still want more!
Tell me please what is it for?

You're a model of respectability,
A pillar of society.
With but only one small vice,
To destroy this Earth – for the *highest price*!

Our Earth is but a garden sealed,
A jewel in space, set on a velvet field.
With so many species lost and dying,
We say: "No more!" yet you keep trying
To kill them off one by one,
For our children they will all be gone.

So do not weep when you see
Your grave beneath a lavatory,
Just read the epitaph and do not fuss,
It will say: "We're just serving you, what you've served us."

Aberdare
September 1989

The Destroyer (*Or, We Are All Guilty*)

She cared for them, She nurtured them,
She gave them all she could.
She felt them playing,
On the mountains, in the meadows, in the woods.

She had a family,
Yet Her children went their separate ways.
Developed in perfect harmony with Her
Through millennia, years, months, weeks and days.

Then one day a child came,
A strange and wondrous sight,
Somewhat conscious of himself,
Not knowing wrong from right.

As he grew,
He began to revel in his mind,
Using it to unlock Her Secrets,
Never knowing what he'd find.

He takes what he wants,
Discards what he doesn't need,
He soon becomes conscious
Of his all-consuming *Greed!*

So he takes Her,
And he rapes Her,
As defenceless She lies;
Uncaring of Her pain,
Ambivalent as She *dies*!

Do I hear you cry: "Who is this cad?
This man so mad!
What is his name?
What is his race?"
Just look in the mirror,
And there you'll see his face.
Beautiful or ugly,
It's the same sight.
Called Mankind,
The ultimate in lethal might!

Aberdare
September 1989
(Post reading "Stark" by Ben Elton)

The Mercenaries Hymn

Beyond the reach of caverns vast,
Atop the highest, most sturdy mast,
Lives a man who sings for his past,
As in loneliness he pines.
He fought in wars, he wrestled bears,
He drank the finest wines;
Yet now he moans his mournful wail,
And far below an empty pail,
Shows he now slowly dies.

What of my life?
That I have fought
In wars untold and great.
Tell me was it all for naught,
That for silver I was bought,
And with mens lives so freely sport,
With vengeance and with hate?

Trained within the militarily,
to become a mercenary,
Told fighting for his country,
"Dulce et decorum est propatria mori."*
Can he see through this disguise?
It cannot come as a surprise,
Off to war, some poor soul dies,
The consequence of some leader's lies.

Trained for a private army,
Trained to fight so bravely,
Trained to enforce slavery,
To his master's will.
Oil Company's private Army;
He's not fighting for his country,
Yet still deploys his skill.

* "It is good and fitting to die for one's country."

And far atop the highest mast,
Beyond the reach of caverns vast,
Lives a man who sings for his past,
In loneliness he pines.
He fought in wars, he wrestled bears,
He drank the finest wines;
Yet now he moans his mournful wail,
For far below an empty pail,
Shows he too sadly dies.

What of my life?
That I have fought
In wars untold and great.
Tell me that it's not for naught,
That for silver I was bought,
And with mens lives so freely sport,
With vengeance and with hate.

Kidderminster
29th of August 2004

Work

We live and we die
And so we continue,
We eat and we build
Bone, brain and sinew.

The lion he lives
To kill and devour,
His prey fleet of foot,
For they know his power.

Eagle aloft,
Espies his prey,
The rabbit knows sloth
Could mean death this day.

Whether predator or prey,
We work to continue,
To eat and to build,
Bone, brain and sinew.

Birmingham
30th of June 2008

Beware the Darkness

Screaming silent through the caverns,
A bestial, black, fragmented mind,
Down to the local "Tavern"
to slit a throat then dine.
To feast and glut upon the blood
that flows so thick and red.
A razor fang releases food,
an oozing slick, like oil – crude –
to satiate her crawling brood;
for this her prey is bled;
almost until dead.
Then as the gloom
of night's dark doom
retreats before the sun's the great bloom,
this great black mind congeals.
And forms outside the caverns cave;
soon to be silent as the grave;

the brood for whom she sups is saved;
The victim's wounds now heal.
Saved by the rising sun,
but his nightmare goes on and on,
to start again when Apollo's gone.
This battle that,
  – the Vampire Bat,
    – has already won.

Birmingham
31st of October 2007

Alex's Love Poem To His Girlfriend

My darling I do miss you so,
This my love you should know,
This time and distance makes love flow,
And grow and grow and grow and grow…

I love you more and more each day,
With all I do and all I say,
I love you in each and every way,
Each day, by day, by day, by day…

This time apart makes our love flow,
Each thought of you makes my heart glow,
For you my love, my love now grows,
And flows and flows and flows and flows…

Know my love I do not jest,
For my love you are the best,
And I know that I am blessed,
As I test and test and test the rest!

Val d'Isere
December 2005

This poem was written by request for one Alex X; an ex-world cup ski racer who was ski teaching and race coaching in France. He is still probably there. His sexual exploits were legendary; women simply fell into his bed – all beautiful and often in groups of varying sizes. He was always very, very honest with them and they simply accepted his ways. On several occasions he tried to move women out of his apartment and into other people's because he met some other girl during the week, that day, or had prior arrangements with other females who were coming to stay with him. A charismatic individual nicknamed "Mr Square", due to his five foot six frame and "medicinally" improved physique, which also enhanced his sexual prowess. He claimed to be able to have sex for hours, and judging by the callers at his door queuing up to get back into his bed his claims seem to have validity. As he once quoted:

"Sex is the business, and business is good."

The above lines communicate something of his style, openness and honesty. No doubt if he has not decided to change his ways, "business is still good."

Supermodel
– In Homage to Attila the Stockbroker's Poem of the Same Title

Attila, Attila what a guy!
Sees through the hell of the adman's lies!
The pain and grief of the *fashionists* creed,
destroying womanhood to fulfil their need,
to create a coathanger that walks around,
a skeleton that counts ounces for pounds.
Great power has the fashion industry
to manipulate minds in our society.
A real man wants a woman he can see!
A companion he can run with, swim or ski-
down a white snowy mountain, in harmony.

At one with Life, free from the death
of the strife brought on by her next breath.
"Will I get heavier, will it make me fat?"
The thinner the thicker,
the sadder the sicker!
All to please The Model Maker,
much sooner to see The Undertaker!
I respect a woman with strength in her thighs,
a powerhouse, an athlete, a huntress who rides,
a great outdoors girl with Life in her eyes!
Strength in her arms,
and clever and wise.
Eats only the best
to fuel her insides,
to stay strong in Heart
and *all else* besides!

Seeing the beauty of grace in her walk,
of Life in her limbs and a brain which can talk.
(The brain's made of fat – it *needs* to be fed!
Not starved by a model halfway brain-dead.)
So, yeah.......... *"Let's get real!"*
And see women that strike
a blow for survival in
this *Jungle of Life*!
Women that strut,
with power and strength!
Like a tigress in rut, *Magnificent!*
Let's see goddesses of sport,
and dancers with grace!
Those who are a credit
to our human race!
Women who are –
healthy, whole –
and happy to *Be*
the perfection –
that they are –
Naturally!

Harpenden
24th of September 2006

Jealousy

Jealousy is a poison, with no rhyme or reason,
That gathers in a small and vital part.
It attacks a man's compassion, destroys all virtuous action,
For Jealousy is a poison of the heart.

And as it builds within a man
Or any living thing,
It destroys all satisfactions
That life does kindly bring.

And if a man weakly goes
Where this poison does dictate,
Then inside and out he will know
The true meaning of hate.

For as he acts on its command
To steal, to lie, to cheat,
It is himself he has damned,
His own strength and virtue beat.

Jealousy is a poison,
A torment of the mind
But who can be at fault
When this poison we do find?

For in our little lives
With their many little things,
Why should we indulge in strife,
When others seem as kings?

Look at the greater picture,
At Sun and Moon and Sky
And simply ask a question,
This question being: "Why?"

Why should we feel this pain
At a friend's deserved success?
When we all may truly gain
From this one who seems so blessed.

He's had a good idea,
From this comes so much wealth!
Fleming's fame and fortune
Brought so many their good health.

Or Einstein with his atom,
Or Edison his light,
Or Newton with his apple,
Or Ali in a fight.

Yet in their time they each did meet,
Such men who sought to kill,
The wonders that they brought to all,
By their sweat, blood and skill.

So as you go upon your way
And meet so many who
Have laboured night and day,
To bring such gifts to you,

For all the things they've done,
They may be deemed as great;
Just respect them and you've won
And vanquished Jealousy – which leads to hate.

Thank them for their efforts,
And the benefits they bring,
Then you will have beaten Jealousy,
And my friend, you'll be a king!

But if you are its servant,
Or its willing slave,
Then you'll be bound in weakness,
From the cradle to the grave.

Val d'Isere
April 2004

"When One Innocent Dies the World Dies"

As the daylight fades
to night's dark shades,
and the gallows justice swings,
the black beaked beasts
of the wing,
unto each new feast
now scream and sing,
fair thanks to Death,
with all their breath,
their beloved and cherished king.

As the blood congeals –
Death's royal seal –
now authorises dinner.
Man's done his crime,
worse than swine,
now sinners killed a sinner.

Innocent or guilty?
Only God can truly know.
A nation becomes filthy
when a good man stretches rope.

All share the blame,
suffer God's disdain,
when a nation takes an innocent life.
Whether crime or war,
God keeps the score,
a killer nations vile laws
are naught in His Great Sight.

So look into your heart,
and know that you are part
of the death, wrought in your nation's name.
Did you stand against it?
Or just go along with it?
– This murder in your name.
Either way you share in it;
your nation will be seen as Gits;
for life is not a *simple* game.

The free will to choose,
to win or lose,
but just what makes a winner?
A heartbeat's heard by God's Good Word,
forced death makes you the sinner.

So good people of all fair lands,
have your rulers put blood on your hands?
Have you taken life?
Have your leaders lied to you?
It's all some politicians do!
And that some profit from strife.

Birmingham
June 2008

After President Barrak Obama's speech in Cairo on the
fourth of June, 2009, I realised that this poem should be
included. I was still looking for a title for the piece and found
one within the words of President Obama. And what
wonderful words they were.

The Messenger

What fantastic things The Prophets did say,
talking about the Judgement Day.
To walk a path and follow a way,
keeping on keeping on, day by day.

To hold on tight – not let go,
to sacrifice so we may know,
to flow and grow so we may glow,
within God's mind a seed now sown.

Brought to fullness by His Light.
Through tempest, grief, toil and strife;
to grow by day and by night
and live forever in God's Sight.

O Prophets – blessings be upon you,
by God's Will He worked through you,
for you were perfect, pure and true,
no matter what they tried to do.

To kill you and those who believed in you,
and the message that He sent through you.
They Knew you were His through and through,
yet kill you is all they tried to do!

But they could not darken the Light
of words which illuminate my heart by night.
For you fought to spread God's Holy Light,
to awaken minds of blackest night,
they saw the light
yet some took fright,
unable to stand against such might,
of words so pure and true and right,
so sure and new, of such delight,
their souls like mine did take flight,
when your words upon them did alight;
giving them such clear insight
to make their own holy fight,
against the ignorance of their plight
and thru knowledge set their hearts alight;
so before God they will be alright.

Their minds erupted with pure love,
They knew you were sent from Him above,
A blinding light, a snow white dove,
A Viceroy of His Perfect Love.

To tell them of The Judgement Day,
to enlighten them, so they all may,
be one with Him through what you say,
For God Is Great – in Every Way.

Birmingham
11th October 2006

J. C.

"The father who dwells within me,
Dwells within you.
The miracles I do
You can do too
But greater than I."
Ascended on high…
Does He tell the truth,
Or is it a lie?
I ask myself: "Why?"

Why should this good man,
With nothing to gain
Do all that he can
And suffer such pain?

Upsetting the Order
Of Social Control,
Who deemed it a Sin
To speak out so bold.

The intellectual rules the social,
Or so it is said
But the mob mind would sooner see
The intellectual dead.

And in this case
It is blatantly clear
That the social succeeded
To kill one so dear.

Not guilty of any real crime,
By His judge an innocent man!
Yet the social behaved like ignorant swine,
To kill Him – as they still can.

A man murdered by a mob,
To quench a vile lust.
From all of us they did rob,
A life so wise and just.

And just what teachings
Could He have told
As He grew wiser,
As He grew old?

What miracles would He have done?
What wonders great and meek?
Where would His kind teachings gone,
Had He but the time to speak?

To tell all that had gone before,
And how he walked His way,
Or simply how He stayed so sure,
Each and every day.

His right to teach and give so much
Was stolen from the rest of us.
By those weak minds full of fear,
And by the lunacy of fixed ideas.

So socially we're all aware,
That each of us must take a care,
To stand against this vile crime
And let live such teachers so sublime.

Those who too have walked a way.
Kept true of heart each day by day.
For from their path they did not stray.
Kept on keeping on – or so they say.

Should He speak or stay in silence?
It is so hard to say.
Would He meet again such violence,
And repeat Golgotha Day?

Is society ready,
To hear it all once more?
Why repeat the obvious,
And can anyone add more?

"Love The Lord thy God with all thy heart,
And thy neighbour as thyself."
It seems so simple, yet it's so hard,
To work this on oneself?

But give it a go, so we will know,
It is the way we might succeed,
To overcome vice and poverty,
And war and hate and Greed...

Should His like return again,
And people make the same mistake,
Will we stand and stop a vile crime,
Or sit grinning at His wake?

Or will there finally be,
The glimmering of sanity,
In our new improved society,
That is safe at last for one like He?
I guess we'll have to wait and see.

Val d'Isere
4th of March 2004

"The highest order of mind is accused of folly, as well as the lowest. Nothing is thoroughly approved but mediocrity. The majority has established this, and it fixes its fangs on whatever gets beyond it either way." – Pascal

Taking Pascal's insight into account it becomes possible to see why Jesus Christ was crucified and Barabas set free. Jesus Christ was as far away from the average as it is possible to get. Barabas was regrettably much closer to the group norm. Being good or bad is irrelevant in this instance, as what matters to the mob/social/emotional mind is that which is most similar to the collective mean. As Barabas was closer to this, it was he who was selected to live. The Australian habit/saying of *"slashing tall poppies"* exemplifies this point. Those which stand out – for whatever reason – suffer as a consequence; regardless of the fact that they bring great benefits to humanity. This is why society is still slaying its saints and letting the devils run amok.

"The world hates a smart arse and loves a bastard." Why is this so? Could it be that people who know more than us – for one reason or another – arouse a sense of jealousy, resentment or inadequacy? Uncomfortable feelings are something that all humans detest. As a ski instructor I recall being coached and mentioning these feelings of discomfort when receiving feedback from my teacher. His reply: "Yes I feel the same discomfort also when someone advises me regarding playing the violin, skiing or many other activities. I now welcome that sense of discomfort as I have discovered that I'm going to learn something. It is only a reaction of our ego which deceives us – all the time – and is the root cause of much of the world's ills." And he was right.

The same coach also mentioned that if a baby is not taught to walk on two legs it never learns to walk upright at all. This is clearly exemplified by the case of feral children who have been raised by wild animals; not a single one has ever been found walking upright as we do, and they all have to be taught how to do it when found – with varying degrees of success. If such a basic ability needs to be communicated to us for us to be able to do it, then it stands to reason that much of what we are is due solely to society teaching us all that we know, *and our willingness to learn*. Before we can know something we must first acknowledge that we have a need to learn it. It is this admission that we are "lacking" in some way that offends our egos. Even when we have acquired a skill, and someone tries to enlighten us further on the subject, it is possible for these uncomfortable feelings to arise... Like my coach I now heartily welcome these unpleasant feelings because I know I'm going to learn something new. It is a pity that such information was not around at the time of Jesus Christ as the outcome at Golgotha *may* have been different.

However, due to the condition of the people at that time, Jesus did not stand a chance. His fate was sealed before the crowd even expressed themselves.

"Birds of a feather flock together."

Evil [................................Average...........................] Good
        ^   ^
    Barabas   Jesus Christ

Despite the fact that Barabas was a murderer, the people of the time felt that they had more in common with him than the truly Good Man Jesus Christ. Their choice of who to support is a reflection of this. Barabas was closer to the norm so they chose him.

"Mediocrity is excellent to the eyes of mediocre people." –
Joubert

If we were to be faced with such a choice in modern times
which would we choose? Which do we choose? I am
convinced that the population of Jerusalem would today
choose Jesus Christ to have been freed, as the collective
consciousness of the people of Israel has refined itself beyond
the barbarous state of the mob of that earlier time – who felt
they had more in common with a murderer than a truly Good
Man. Any other conclusion is too terrifying to contemplate...

Critically, the key point seems to be: Where does each of us
stand as we go through life day by day, moment by moment?
Do we as individuals free goodness and so abandon evil or
vice versa? Or, put another way, do we stop to think, analyse
and use our intellects, or simply follow the blind impulses of
raw emotion, animal instinct and mob mindlessness?

It is sad and telling that it was the priesthood of that time –
under the direction of Ciaphas the high priest – that
engineered Jesus Christ's fate...

Kleinwalsertal

Kleinwalsertal, ancient home of my heart,
your people and mountains stand set apart.
The goodness and friendship,
the kindness and love,
the closeness and kinship,
they Live God's Good Love.

Folk of the mountains,
honest and true,
decent, courageous,
in all that they do.

I've travelled the world
yet have seldom seen,
folk like the Walsers
who *live* life's great dream.

From skiing at night
beneath the cover of stars
– a heart's true delight –
and with folks straight from Mars.

Warriors true –
in all that they do –
can show us all
a good thing or two.

From climbing, skiing
and surfing on ice,
to simply the view
of this small paradise.

For all these and more,
I do thee adore,
thankful to return
once again to your shore.

For on our journey,
this quest through life,
we have trials and tests,
know toil and strife.

Yet their traditions
shows they are blessed,
their intuition
has helped me to best,
the darkness, confusion
and clouds left by time
and their caring and sharing
is truly divine.

They look after the past
with such dedication,
I saw a subtle, sacred sign
and then asked a question.
"Was this the way to my salvation?"

There at their Church the secret still stands.
Cared for by the faithful,
the true of heart and hand.
Preserved for all, always to see,
the secret that showed – and confirmed – salvation to me.

A sage knew the answer
and hid it on stone.
The faithful preserved it -
and it shows the way Home.

Kleinwalsertal though the world I roam,
you are the home of the Secret
which shows a way Home.
There in your art,
preserved, set apart,
the Secret that made me *at Home in my heart.*

Birmingham
19 August 2008

A Vision

In meditation I did see,
as my vision did take flight,
a journey and a prophecy
of the lights within the night.

I saw the Earth from way above,
on a still and perfect night.
This perfect planet, which I love,
with ne'er a storm, nor cloud in sight.
Saw all the lands alive with lights,
Every inch a sad delight.
Humanities numbers greater,
than any other on our home,
this once perfect planet,
now only ours to roam.
Humanity had eaten all,
till all that's left was stone.

Poland* was the first,
as the lights started to fade.
Then one by one the lights went out,
as there were no new babies made.

* Or it could be Belorus

Western Europe followed next,
but that's not where it ended.
More rapidly, than I could see,
the night to Earth descended.

The cities all went deathly quiet,
their lights once bright did fade,
as the glow, from down below
turned into night's dark shade.

Russia and the Arab lands,
India and the Islands,
American North and South,
lost the lights within the night,
as humanity checked out.

The Hotel was now bankrupt,
all its creatures dead.
The plants had gone,
As we did wrong,
and we'd not any bread.

The hotel had been poisoned,
by the fools who made the rules.
They sold the rights to license life,
now we were suffering like mules.

We'd sold our children's children,
to put petrol in a car.
And made their lives what we despise,
for food they went to war.

But when the war was over,
humanity was gone.
And the cannibals that ate the meat
died as Time moved on.

Our children were all sterile
and turned to us to say:
"By our Merciful, Loving Lord!
You were warned it would end this way!

You let the madmen rule you.
Those evil, lying swines,
you let those Gits
get away with it,
now it's us who are left to die!

You let them bind you with their rules,
which they decreed as laws,
now we are all like mules
and the fault of it is yours!

You stayed a simple placid sheep
as the 'Good Shepherd' took you in,
now you have the cheek to stand and weep,
it's weakness that's your sin!

Too weak for an opinion,
too weak to voice your views,
you were just a minion
of the men that broke the rules!

What of the Laws of Mother Nature?
You knew them well enough!
With your Weakness you Betrayed Her!
To your Mother you're a Traitor!
You befouled Her then you raped Her,
just to make a buck!

What of the life I could have had?
Been a mother, **been a dad!**
The joy to have my own child sing this song!
To tell me I was weak and wrong.
And as Time unfolds,
look after me as I grow old…

I want my own child,
more than I can say!
But your greed and idleness
took that right away!

Without a thought for me or mine
you just let them do their thing.
Well dear Mum, dear Dad,
It's now time for me to sing:

You sold me to a politician,
a lying lawyer louse,
a puppet of big business,
The bank will always own the house!

The government was a sham,
politicians were a joke.
With all that wealth and technology
how could anyone be broke?

You were servants of The System,
of Slavery and Tax.
So the bankers and *their* friends
could kill you and relax.

Kill you in *their* wars.
They own both the teams,
own the countries, own the towns,
and the Arms factories!
Who cares what the score is,
It's Peace that is our Dream!
A planet fit to live in,
within which all life teems!......"

****

I had a dream this very morn,
which left me sad and so forlorn,
of what our children had to say,
when the lawyers licensed life away.

****

*This is a potential future. It is what could await our
descendants if humanity – as a whole – fails to treat this
glorious corner of creation with the decency, respect and
thankfulness our incredible home deserves. All the growth
brought about by our hard won advances could be lost, and
we disappear. This is the natural result of unrestrained greed,
cowardice and compliance, and nothing else. Dare you make
a stand for change? Dare you not?*

Birmingham
1st of October 2006

Saladin Ruminates

Though we seem quite different,
From realms set far apart,
In Truth we are in Union,
Through His Love within our hearts.
And I am sure you see,
For we exist beyond Space and Time;
Beyond the concepts of this rhyme;
And One in Union so sublime,
For all eternity –
  As we –
   Are One with He –
Who flows through the Light
And is one with all things,
He is the Great Source to whom my heart sings.
I Love our Creator who gives us our wings.

Now my reflector,
Beyond all conjecture,
My self annihilator,
My Father, my Mother,
My soul's truest lover,
For there can be no other
Of whom my heart sings.

Though we seem quite distant,
We are One within our hearts.
In *Truth* not for an instant
Can we ever be apart.

Le Havre
April 2007

GOD – The Most Merciful

GOD – The Most Merciful,
In times of great sorrow,
with His Love in our hearts
we know a better tomorrow.
By the mistakes which we make
from day-to-day
He allows us to take
much wiser ways.
He helps us to grow
and also to know
as we experience in life His merciful flow.
By what we receive and what we do
Gods mercy flows to and onwards through you.

Birmingham
November 2007

GOD – The Maker of Order

The Maker of Order – The Giver of Life,
by God's Great Direction
All Flows with Perfection;
but abuse of free will – through selfishness – strife.
The functions of all depend on each other,
abundance flows freely when all are as brothers.
Yet *one* filled with *greed*,
leaves others in need
by the foul fruits from this *Satan seed*…..

The goodness in nature,
when things take their course,
is a Perfect Teacher
– is God's Greatest Preacher;
and he who takes heed,
from error is freed
knowing harmony, peace and justice indeed.

Birmingham
November 2007

GOD – The Holy One Free from All Blemishes

GOD – The Holy One Free from All Blemishes.
He who bestows, heals, supports and replenishes.
When faith may waver He leads and refreshes,
as the world and its ways become our great nemesis.
As temptation arises,
and doubts creep in;
as Satan conspires
your soul to win;
and feelings like fire
compel you to sin;
and with a burning desire
you want to give in;
yet God's Love in your heart
means you are a part
of the Holy One's Grace,
His blessing and favour,
turn to God's Love for He is our saviour;
and the flames and fire
of hellish desire
are cooled by the heart
and simply depart.

Birmingham
November 2007

171

God – Who Judges All

He is the cause of the judged, the judge, the justice and the
judgement.
Who to His creation gives His consent;
the faithful and worthy to Heaven are sent,
and wrongdoers receive Just punishment.

One must meet the cause to receive the effect.
To His Teachers and Prophets show true respect.
For they show the way one's soul to protect,
So upon Judgement Day you will not be rejected,
and will instead have your soul collected.

How do you see your own destiny?
For it's an effect of a cause with a quantified quality.
Which cannot be changed, or be rearranged,
for all is predestined, where cause leads to effect
The perfect "reward" that God does direct.

Yet God in his mercy has shown us the Light.
Through books like the Bible, which guide us aright.
So His Laws and Commands are not forgot.
We comprehend them by knowledge and sincerity,
wisdom and purity,
faith and capacity,
and finally our lot.

There are the practical who try to be ready,
through what they have learned from lessons already;
by what happened before, to what happens after,
they have a healthy concern for their own hereafter.

Then there are those who repent and regret,
the problems they've caused to those they have met.
They thank God for the good here in their lives,
and the things they can do to help others to thrive.

Then there are those who live in the now;
unheeding the "why", "where", or "how";
they try to live right by God's Commands;
knowing He has All in His Good Hands.

Blessed are those who are unconcerned,
with past, present or future for they have learned,
their hearts taken up by the splendour of God;
they are always with Him – Our Loving Lord.

Then there are those,
whom God has chose'
a channel to be
for others' destiny.
And if a man in purity,
peace of mind and tranquillity,
his prayers recites,
in the middle of the night,
in his sleep he will know God's Light and Delight,
and in this *Good* time,
will gain knowledge sublime,
as his heart is filled by Love Divine.

Birmingham
30th of June 2008

God – The Opener

When things seem tied in a knot
 – whether friends or possessions,
places or professions –
He is The Easer of all that is rigid and locked.

Hearts filled with sadness
or minds full of doubt,
with answers to questions
we can't figure out,
God – The Opener – opens them All
through our good deeds, no matter how small.

No other can open the secrets within –
Your heart – His House – the key is with Him.
Help those who have fallen in all that you do,
and should you fall others will in turn help you.
By *always* being gentle, loving and kind
you will unlock His Blessings, His Mercy
and possess peace of mind.

* "He Who Opens For Others" – is he who has risen to perfection
by his selfless ways and dedication.
He can solve any and all the problems of others
and does so with ease seeing all men as brothers.
With such secret knowledge God grants him the key,
and he can in turn set any man free.
This man who by action has so many served,
receives God's special bounties which are normally reserved.

Their sincere thanks to The Bringer of Benefits,
without any conditions or limits.
Asking naught in return for there is nothing He needs
and so from hardship we are then freed.
Often done in an incredible way,
so we can bear witness
and have something to say,
of God's Perfect Goodness
day after day.
War, poverty, ignorance and being enslaved,
 – these are some of the hardships from which we are saved.
So we can now flow
in His Loving Way,
giving to others
 – our brothers –
so they too are okay.

* "Giver of God's Will"
One who gives just what God wishes;
infinite gifts he/she freely dispenses;
to those who are worthy – with no objection;
they reflect into the world God's Giving Perfection.

Birmingham
November 2007

God – The Giver of Peace

The Freer from Distress;
a blessing to others, for which we're then blessed.
This light in our heart,
when it shines like the sun,
all distress will depart,
all pain will be gone;
For His Love is a Light,
the Power of Life – banishing strife –
His peace flows on and on.

God's blessing flows through you from heaven above,
and from brother to brother,
now one in God's Love.
"Shalom aleykem." –
"Aleykum salaam."
More than a greeting,
God shines through each man.

Birmingham
November 2007

God – The Crusher

GOD – The Crusher
Who controls all things,
Destroyer of nations, Breaker of kings.
In His Infinite Power none can escape Him,
all the Heavens and Hells bow down before Him.
Those lost in sin
– a person or nation –
will know God always wins
as they harvest destruction.
Treachery, deceit, tyranny, arrogance
the sins of dark rulers living in Ignorance.
To those in such darkness His power is sent;
destroyed when they baulk at the chance to repent.
Purifying creation so it may be perfected,
halting such vice
– so others think twice –
and worldliness fight,
and on Judgement Day in Heaven accepted.

* "Soldier of God"
This is the name God's Warriors know;
conquering self and ones evil ego.
Enslaving the enslaver
he fights His Great Fight,
becoming all-powerful to do that which is right.

Birmingham
November 2007

God Who Constricts, God Who Relieves

God constricts, God releases.
Both serve His Will these complimentary phases.
When He Closes His Hand
All blessings may cease;
wealth becomes poverty,
health turns to disease
and the happiest heart loses its ease.

When He Opens His Hand,
all blessings due
flow unto us
like a tidal wave through
the blocks and constrictions
within our lives,
our attitudes, afflictions
and even our minds
– for God is Perfection and He is Kind.

He helps us to grow with His Love and Light,
To know Him and give Him true love and delight.
For as we – the created – go through Creation,
we can bare witness to God's Perfect Perfection.

...I believe we can all gain salvation,
for we're all part of God, in this, His Creation;
man, woman and child, and every nation.
His Sparks in our heart,
for of Him we're a part
of His Infinite Perfection,
in manifestation.
Which path to choose? Our only question.

The world we lose with our last breath.
The Eternal then opens upon our death.
So it is wise to prepare,
because we are all going there.
With a heart full of love
– to Heaven above.
But one filled with hate
– of self or another –
Will open Hell's gates
– which will you know my brother?

God is all Merciful and life is a test.
He tries us with trials He knows we can best;
Patience is one, in times of constriction.
In such dark days let faith be our companion.

For by knowing His ways, your faith is a glue,
that binds you to Him and He unto you.
So one day soon you'll *know* He is Love
as He smiles within you, and you become His Beloved.

Yet when he grants you comfort and bliss,
times of abundance, unrivalled success,
all kinds of treasure,
plentiful pleasure,
remember you are His,
and avoid all excess;
for this too is one of His tests;
sent to examine your faith
– and thankfulness.
So when such times should come and go,
take care and beware the deceits of the Ego.
For your ego will whisper such sweet, selfish words;
claiming your success and security is yours not the Lord's.
Send praises to God and remember His Name,
stay humble and modest and avoid Satan's Shame.*
In both states stay stable,
for life is a game –
depression or mania the result is the same.
By losing our balance we can lose our way;
losing the lessons that matter today.
So accept with good grace – whatever God's pleasure
(and also the *wisdom* – His *Heaven sent Treasure).*

* The Sin of Arrogance

"Those Who Open by God's Will" – give very generously,
what they possess, they pass on quite freely.
Like Angels of Love, sent from above,
they bring joy to the hearts of Gods Beloveds.
Inner and outer, abundant in light;
in them manifested this secret of life;
bringing outside, what lies deep within
themselves and others and staying free of all sin.

Birmingham
November 2007

God – The Sovereign

God – The Sovereign
who in Heaven does Reign.
By His Will
– we have free will
to know pleasure or pain.
He sends down His blessings
by loss or by gain,
– for in the end, it is all the same.
His is the Kingdom,
Eternal and Pure
and He grants us the freedom
to choose which we want more;
this world – which we will one day depart –
or His Heaven Eternal – whose key lies in our hearts.

Birmingham
November 2007

God – Who Sees and Hears All

God the Seer,
He sees all that has been,
and all that will be
and all that there is across Eternity.
From the time before Time,
when He stirred the Sea
of Nothingness from which arose all galaxies
and all universes across Infinity.

He sees everything in Time
until after Judgement Day
and all that happens in every way.
He has given sight to us in his creation,
Phenomenal yet limited in its perception.
We see only objects in a limited space,
unable to see beyond this confined place.
Our sight is limited and we cannot see Him,
yet He sees what we do and what goes on within
our hearts and our minds in every detail,
and if we follow His Prophets we will never fail
to please our creator and never sin,
and he who sees and knows himself
knows that God sees him.

So to know life beyond Life,
Eternal Heavenly bliss,
is simply to know we're a creation of His.
When you stand before a brother
can he see into your heart?
This one who is another,
distinct and apart.
He cannot know your motives or needs,
so judges you only by your outer deeds.

Yet God who created you and all before,
He who protects you, sustains you,
Loves you and more,
gives you all that you have,
or could ever wish for;
Yes, your Creator,
The One I Adore.

He who is without and within you
by night and by day;
He is closer to you
than your jugular vein;
He who feels all your pleasure,
And all your Pain...

Every moment of your life know He can See;
this one you depend on for Eternity;
yet in front of His eyes without fear or respect
do you tell lies or His teachings reject?
Is it because you cannot see Him
that you believe God The All Seeing can't see you sin?

(All Hearing)

He is the One Who Hears All Things,
the thoughts of our minds,
the grasshopper that sings,
the beating of all butterflies wings,
the rustle of leaves blown by the wind.

He hears the growing of plants,
the footsteps of ants,
the scuff of the dancers' feet as they dance,
the meteors and comets hurtling through space,
and what's felt in the hearts of the whole human race;
the accelerations of atoms as they move through the void,
and He definitely hears when one is destroyed!

He hears every voice, in every tongue,
and the voice of our conscience when we're doing wrong.
All things heard each as clear as the other.
There's a reason for this, my sister my brother;
all is registered, responded to and understood,
the guilty are punished,
He rewards the good;
and when a soul to heaven does cry,
the call is heard and then satisfied.

He hears All without distraction.
Those with ears to hear,
show an attribute of His perfection.
There are none like Him in this manifestation.
Any who seem so are just a reflection,
a means, a method, a path to understand,
His Truth in creation,
a guide for salvation,
One we can walk with in peace hand-in-hand.

Those who truly See and those who truly Hear,
Are those to whom God draws near.
They become the eyes He sees with,
the ears with which He hears,
becoming more loving and wise as they grow in years.

Birmingham
June 2008

One last thought:

*"Just as God gave different fingers to the hand, so gave
He different religions to the world."* – Genghis Khan

Acknowledgement

Special thanks must go to Her Majesty Queen Elizabeth The Second, His Royal Highness Prince Charles The Prince of Wales and Lord and Lady Coleridge, whose kind words helped me to keep on keeping on, etc.

I would also like to thank all those great groups who played at "Mothers – The Home of Good Sounds" for all the groundbreaking music; along with the managers John Taylor, Gary Surman and John Singer, plus promoter Phil Myatt.

Many thanks to all the people and good friends who generously gave their time, kindness, hospitality, inspiration and encouragement with the book: Dan and Caroline Burton, Pat and Ralph Wills, Peter Hawkins, Guy Hawkins, Cyril Manning, Justin Ireland, Alan Stevenson OBE, Bethan Myfanwy Hughes, Josie Penzer, Sylvie and Christian Tessandier, Steve Tidbury, Terry Drayton, Richard Whitmarsh, Kevin and Colleen Taylor, Maryam Mafi, Bob, Hilda and Nigel Wall, George Zych, plus my fellow cultural representatives on the 'World Showcase', along with the staff and Imagineers at EPCOT Center, Walt Disney World, to name but a few – plus all those who gave inspiration for a poem.

Of course I have to thank Miles and Kath for putting up with me, along with their kindness, generosity and for simply believing in the early days.

I'd also like to thank some other significant people in my life including Professor James McKusick Ph.D. for agreeing to write the foreword for this book, and of course the Friends of Coleridge, plus the academic community as a whole for preserving, identifying and classifying such masterpieces as 'Kubla Khan' etc; along with all the teachers, mentors, masters and professionals I have ever had the privilege to study and work with; Such as: Apuna, Thierry Pruvost, Alex Scattergood, David Rubens, Phil Campion, Lee Sansum, Lee Mathews and all the colleagues and friends from my military days. Notably: Brigadier Michael Calvert DSO (and bars), Lawrence Hay, Lance Lindsay, Kev "Big 80" Roberts, Aidan Rice, Mark J. Adams RGJ, Philip Sybeth, Saud bin Badr al Busaidi, Tony Williams, Dave Miller, Steve Lawrence, Simon Garratt, Greg and Sally Heath, Dom and Susie Potter plus all other friends and "foes" alike – thanks for the education.

I have to thank the Sufi and Sant Mat poets, His Holiness The Dalai Lama and Es Sayyid Es Shaykh Tanner Ansari – along with all the Teachers and Prophets of the world's religions (peace be upon them).

Plus Louis Walsh for passing on what was required here in the world, and the team at Stargate Atlantis, who were playing on the TV as I wrote the final forty lines to 'Kubla Khan'. Also Mr Kelly, Miss Jordan and Mrs Buntin – my English teachers from school days.

Finally, the Rev Simon Franklin, the churchwarden and ladies of Ottery St Mary's Church, for their kind and generous assistance on the night of the recital on the fourth of July 2008.

God bless you all.

About the Author

Russell Lee Hawkins is an ex-British Army officer, internationally qualified ski teacher, bodyguard, kung fu teacher and is currently exploring the realms of performance poetry. He is well travelled, having resided, worked and/or trained in the following countries: England, Wales, Scotland, Ireland, Germany, France, Italy, Egypt, Israel, Taiwan, Hong Kong, India, Malaysia, Thailand, U.S.A., Australia, New Zealand, etc. Further information can be seen on his web site at: www.rlhawkins.co.uk

Cover note

Xanadu (Sheng-du – the luxurious palace of Kubla Khan) is associated with Shambala and Shangri-La, rumored to be mystical places a person may visit to attain "oneness with the infinite". As Stonehenge was a centre of worship and a calendar – dealing with the truths of the universe – it must also be a prime contender for being such a place. One only has to visit to experience a sense of peace, tranquillity and "connection to the all". So as such it is a Shangri-La, a Shambala, a Xanadu... an Avalon...